Coaching Youth Sports

Coaching Youth Sports

Guidelines to Ensure Development of Young Athletes

Charlie Sullivan

ROWMAN & LITTLEFIELD
Lanham • Boulder • New York • London

Published by Rowman & Littlefield
An imprint of The Rowman & Littlefield Publishing Group, Inc.
4501 Forbes Boulevard, Suite 200, Lanham, Maryland 20706
www.rowman.com

6 Tinworth Street, London, SE11 5AL, United Kingdom

Copyright © 2022 by Charlie Sullivan

All rights reserved. No part of this book may be reproduced in any form or by any electronic or mechanical means, including information storage and retrieval systems, without written permission from the publisher, except by a reviewer who may quote passages in a review.

British Library Cataloguing in Publication Information Available

Library of Congress Cataloging-in-Publication Data

Names: Sullivan, Charles, 1968– author.
Title: Coaching youth sports : guidelines to ensure development of young athletes / Charles Sullivan.
Description: Lanham, Maryland : Rowman & Littlefield, 2022. | Summary: "A coach will learn the science of how a player learns and techniques to be used to increase motivation"— Provided by publisher.
Identifiers: LCCN 2021027506 (print) | LCCN 2021027507 (ebook) | ISBN 9781475860030 (cloth) | ISBN 9781475860047 (paperback) | ISBN 9781475860054 (epub)
Subjects: LCSH: Sports for children—Coaching.
Classification: LCC GV709.24 .S85 2022 (print) | LCC GV709.24 (ebook) | DDC 796.083—dc23
LC record available at https://lccn.loc.gov/2021027506
LC ebook record available at https://lccn.loc.gov/2021027507

To my wife Maggie
Through my coaching journey there have been many times when you needed to coach alone at home. Your support and encouragement to take advantage of these amazing professional growth opportunities was essential and appreciated. Thanks, for being the captain of our team and being a great coach's wife.

To my kids, Fionnuala, Patrick, and Caeli
Thanks for all your support. The best thing in life is watching you be happy and successful. Here is to always working on a great process.

Contents

Foreword	ix
Preface: Why I Wrote This Book	xiii
Acknowledgments	xix
Introduction	xxi
Chapter 1: Youth Sport Research: What We Know about Youth Sports	1
Chapter 2: How to Structure Your Team: Methods to Set Your Team Up for Success	13
Chapter 3: Winning Is Important, But . . . : Channeling Your Team's Focus to Play at Their Best	21
Chapter 4: The Science about How Players Learn: What We Know about Motor Learning	31
Chapter 5: Competition and Deliberate Goals: How to Increase Focus in Your Practice	45
Chapter 6: Communication and Feedback: The Art and Science of How You Should Talk to Players	53
Chapter 7: Coaching Like a Teacher: Strategies That All Great Teachers Use That Will Improve Your Coaching	65
Chapter 8: Reactions to Errors: Let Errors Show Your Players the Path to Improvement	75

Chapter 9: Game Day: Things to Consider When Preparing for
   Competition   81

Chapter 10: Youth Sports in Norway: Are We Moving in the Right
   Direction?   89

About the Author   95

Foreword

If you are a serious athlete and have a passion for a sport, yet you now worry about coaching your child's youth team(s) and the possible nonathletes you think might need the "There's no crying in baseball" lecture, then this is the book for you. Drawing on Charlie's years of coaching experience and wisdom, this book will also help you crystallize your already good practice, learn important aspects of sport psychology, and leave behind the "Hollywood" coaching moments. You will soon be on your way to building your own authentic moments with the young athletes. If you are the nonathlete who did not play much organized sports, and you now find yourself on the way to a coaches meeting for youth soccer, softball, or baseball, then this is the book for you. Or maybe you had growing up a string of some bad coaches or parents who got in over their head and played favorites with the starting lineup instead of teaching skills. Either way, the fact that you picked up this book is a sure sign that you want to do right by your kid and his and her teammates. Moreover, regardless of your background, if you want to add an important ingredient of reflection into your coaching craft, read this book as a way to validate your positive approaches and reach your potential as a coach. Your commitment to your team will benefit from this reflection process, and it will help you unlock each athlete's potential.

    As Charlie's older brother I bring a long and very personal perspective to observing first hand his passion for sports. I know the origin stories that led to each of his coaching accolades. His siblings and I all glow with pride when he wins different coaching awards, yet on some level, we know deep down that he deserved each recognition, and, with a nodding nonchalance, we often tell others that the governing bodies or fellow coaches who are bestowing these awards are just catching up to what we already know. Charlie was born to coach! Charlie's ability to get to know his players and their obstacles inspires him to push each individual team member to his potential. In the end, Charlie's passion produces results. Just look up his winning percentage. Or his record eleven National Championship Titles. That said, his 2015 USA Volleyball's All-Time Great Coach award really did raise some eyebrows in the family. But really, all you need to know are a few Old Testament stories from his youth.

When Pablo Picasso was trying to share with the world insights about art education, he emphasized that "Every child is an artist. The problem is how to remain an artist once he grows up." When it comes to Charlie's approach to sports, getting to know his players, and working with them in practice and competition, not much has changed. He carries all the important enthusiastic wonders of an inspired child. He is still an inspiring child at heart! He is still the one everyone wants in the circle of players. What better advocate is there than someone like Charlie whose personality and general disposition exhibits Emerson's idea of "perpetual youth." Sure, younger siblings all across the land gained the respect of older siblings and athletes in an authentic pick-up environment, gathered immeasurable moments of future grit, and became better simply by playing up in age range and size with older brother's friends. But how many of those younger siblings actually learned how to find the joy of practicing? How many of them initiated their own skills development? How many taught their young selves in their own mind and spirit the ability to believe in themselves?

Charlie and I share the middle of a large family, and his older siblings and I all remember how neighbors used to go out of their way to share their impressions of Charlie to my parents. These were fun chats and they often remarked about Charlie playing baseball in the middle of the street when he was six and seven years old. He was too young to travel a distance to a baseball field at a school. While my parents entered into many different conversations about their six kids, they enjoyed these anecdotes because more people went out of their way—even the retired folks living on the streets who didn't like our loud games. Everyone was always taken by Charlie's serious and joyful sense of play. Now, there are different versions of this story depending on the sport, but to keep with the baseball theme, Charlie would play with my friends and me in our pick-up games' baseball games. When we finished and started a new activity or switched to riding bikes the way young boys resemble pack animals, Charlie would get left behind. Nevertheless, he would happily take the bat, which was too big for him at the time, and practice hitting a baseball down the center of our dead-end street. Lugging a large, wooden bat that was almost as tall as he was, Charlie would toss the ball into the air and find the belief that enabled him to swing a large bat that rivaled his height and connect with the ball. After the ball cracked off the bat, he would gaze the tattered baseball's trajectory through the arch bows of our tree-lined street and then walk to pick up the ball and do it all again. We lived in a Long Island development that was famous for the angle of its dead-end streets, and traffic was successfully limited to only those who lived on the street. So, Charlie could and would repeat this practice for hours. And everyone knew Charlie's big beaming face and was on the lookout for him at any time of the day as he consistently practiced hitting baseballs up and down our dead-end road with a smile on his face. And my friends would wonder with me, "Why does your brother waste his time chasing balls down the road," which was a good question back then when you think of how our steps in those days were counted with the opposite intention than today's step craze, and actually going after a ball was something you did as a punishment in a game. Or to use the vernacular of the day, you had to take "loser steps" when your opponent knocked it over your head. What we didn't realize at the time was that Charlie reinterpreted these steps at a very young age.

When we moved from Long Island to a leafy neighborhood in New Jersey, we were fortunate to be a few blocks and a walk through the woods where we ended up behind Drew University's soccer field. In the late 1970s and early 1980s, Drew University had a competitive soccer program, and watching these giants play up close when we were little was impressive. We all signed up for the summer soccer camps that hosted other college coaches and key players we got to know from watching their seasons. While we all fell in love with the game of soccer through playing and watching these athletes, Charlie created a special bond when he went through their camp. The team essentially adopted him while he was in fifth and sixth grade as a playing mascot and allowed him to sit on the bench during the games and play the warm-ups. By the time Charlie made it to high school, he was a contributing varsity player and captain, which surprised no one in the family. And that point when any high school athlete matures and winnows his/her pick-up sports to a few passion sports, Charlie was busy growing into his athletic director's phase. His high school pick-up sports time would find him organizing all sorts of kids in our neighborhood and around town for games. Then on Sundays, he would work his phone lists and organize street hockey tournaments on our street. So many followed his athletic leadership vision then.

Charlie not only motivates athletes; he also inspires fellow educators. On the eve of a 2015 Springfield College Lacrosse playoff game, Charlie met up with the team and continued the tradition of speaking to most Springfield College teams as they transition to their extended season. His legendary "Winning the Game of Belief" talk buttresses the foundation of his career-winning record and impressively stands as a 24-1 record for the other teams he speaks with as they nervously prepare for post-season competition. Interestingly, one of the players recorded his team's motivational moment after this talk and shared the audio with his father, who is a tenured associate professor at Molloy College. Immediately upon hearing a muffled recording, Kevin Sheehan EdE, a renowned expert on applying positive psychology and growth mindset ideas to teaching and learning environments, partnered with Charlie and shadowed his ensuing Volleyball season. While Kevin Sheehan is himself an internationally recognized coach in the world of lacrosse, the co-authored book speaks to Charlie's ability to collaborate with all sorts of passionate educators. The subsequent text, *Winning the Game of Belief: Cultivating the Cultural Grit that Defines America's Greatest Coaches*, speaks to so many of Charlie's strengths as a passionate coach and educator; it's also a real hard copy of his own sports psychology degree that he learned through his relentless pursuit to understand how to unlock athletic excellence. In other words, the book and partnership with Kevin Sheehan is Charlie's own graduate degree in sports psychology.

Again, you should be congratulated for holding this book in your hands as it means that you appreciate everything sports can teach young people as well as all of the social and emotional learning opportunities on and off the field of play. You should know, too, that you are in good hands learning from Charlie, and this edition is just the latest iteration of his highly successful and passionate career. When reflecting on the nature of vocation, Pablo Picasso also shared with the world insights about art careers when he extolled that "The meaning of life is to find your gift. The Purpose of life is to give it away." Charlie found his gift a long time ago. Whether it was incessantly hitting baseballs up the street and joyfully repeating the steps or whether it was organizing street hockey tournaments. Presently, he infectiously instills that joy and passion into every drill, every practice plan, and into every season. Just ask any number of players on his team now or the numerous ones who return often to Blake Area on the campus of Springfield College every season. While Charlie did not become a professional soccer player after he graduated from college, and he lost a most interesting coin toss, which launched his volleyball career, he did, in the words of his namesake grandfather, "Fall down the stairs and get up with a shave and a haircut." While a repeated phrase at our family dinner table, Charlie internalized the spirit of my grandfather's line. Charlie learned to turn his life's obstacles into positive vocational paths. Charlie came from a supportive family, and neighborhoods that appreciated his love of sports where he began his athletic careers.

Hopefully, the gift of this book's wisdom may help you appreciate every step of your current athletic season. Moreover, the structure and passion in this book will put you on the path for more productive seasons in years to come coaching youth sports.

—William Sullivan, brother, English teacher, and high school coach

Preface: Why I Wrote This Book

For many of you now sporting a whistle around your neck, this might not have been your chosen career path or the way you envisioned spending your weekends. Now that you have the title, coach, and the whistle, what to do might at first seem overwhelming. If that is the case, then this book is for you.

For others of you after storied athletic careers and years of arm chairing quarterbacking, you may feel that this book is one that you do not need. Even if you have coached an elite travel team for years, I am sure there are details that you can work on to improve your coaching. Coaching is a craft that all coaches can spend more time focusing on to make improvements.

MY INTRODUCTION TO COACHING

After my graduation from Springfield College in 1991, I traveled to London, England in hopes of playing soccer on a professional level. Quickly not enjoying much success in soccer, I ran out of money and crawled to the front door of an international school, asking them if I could do some work, any kind of work or manual labor for money.

At that point in my life my goal was to be a full-time soccer player, and I was not seeking a full-time job outside of soccer, but eating did come first. The head of the school responded to my request with an offer. "We don't have any work here but we do have a position for a physical education teacher, coach, and athletic director in our sister school in Rome, the Marymount International School for Girls."

Shortly after my taking the job, the Marymount International School for girls decided to open its enrollment to boys to increase revenue. This addition necessitated the school now sponsoring boys' sports. I took this as a sign that my luck had turned, especially when I learned that one of the new sports to be added was, soccer. The other sport to be added was volleyball.

The idea of coaching soccer might be the opening of a new doorway for me in the face of my rapidly vanishing dreams of being a professional soccer player. The only catch to the soccer job is that I soon discovered that there were two males teaching at the school, and both of us were vying for this one soccer job.

In a meeting with the head mistress, I insisted that there was no way that I was coaching the boys' volleyball team. I had never even seen a volleyball match. I needed to coach soccer. Since my competitor for the position said the same thing, we decided to flip a coin to see who would coach the soccer team and who would coach the volleyball team.

As in a Disney movie, my entire life dramatically seemed to have come down to the flip of this coin. The coin was tossed and the result did change the direction my life, but not in the expected direction. I lost that coin toss and the dreamed of soccer position. This was my introduction to the world of coaching volleyball, a lost coin toss.

I share this story, because you may also share an unexpected transition from player to coach without warning. There are vast differences between the understanding and practices needed to be a successful player and those now needed as a coach. Fortunately, I had attended Springfield College, perhaps the finest preparation school for physical education and coaching in the world. One of Springfield College's many nicknames is "the coaching factory." I had even learned a great deal in an undergraduate coaching course and I had interacted with many great coaches and teachers. I have continued to benefit the last 26 years from the environment at the "teaching school" my entire career.

BEYOND TACTICS: BUILDING ON A FOUNDATION OF SPORTS PSYCHOLOGY

As a teacher coach at Springfield College, I was very fortunate that my department chair took a chance and allowed me to teach Sport Psychology. When I was first assigned this course almost twenty years ago, I had researched and used sport psychology as the newly hired coach of the men's volleyball team at Springfield College. Through these experiences, I already began to fall in love with the topic, yet there were some concerns in the Sport Psychology department about my qualifications for teaching the course. These concerns arose for good reason as I had not earned a degree in the subject area. However, the immeasurable variable that I was able to offer in those department meetings was passion.

I immersed myself in the study of psychology as I came to be passionate about the mind as well as the body. Excited to have a chance to teach the course after a semester of shadowing a fellow colleague, I was surprised to find one of the chapters in the Introduction to Sport Psychology book that I was using titled, Youth Sports.

What did youth sports have to do with sport psychology? I thought sport psychology was really the realm of elite performers in sport seeking to achieve maximum performances. From my naïve perspective, this was not essential for those working with those being introduced to a sport. In this way, the department was correct. I had a lot to learn. The truth is that there may be nothing more vital for youth coaches than a basic understanding of the developmental psychology that defines their players.

I was assigned to teach Sport Psychology at Springfield College in my third year as a professor and head men's volleyball coach at the school. Twenty years later I am fortunate to carry on this role. During this time, I have grown as a teacher and a coach. I have observed and worked with the top coaches in my sport both across the country and around the world at the college and professional levels of play. I wrote this book, in part, because I believe a basic foundation of psychology needs to drive the coaching practices of all coaches, especially youth coaches!

What truly drove me to write this book was that when I observed the coaches of my three children, who participated in a wide variety of youth sports throughout their childhoods and teen years, I have seen little understanding of the psychological needs of the children that they coach in place. In dabbling with the coaching some of these teams myself, I have come to experience how great an impact a well-planned practice makes on youth sports.

What I have learned from all of these experiences is that understanding the psychology of youth sports is essential for youth sports leaders today so that coaches can provide their athletes with the most beneficial experience possible. In my own life, I have become more passionate than ever about coaching and how important sport psychology is for athletes of all ages and levels, especially for the participants in youth sport.

The motivation for writing this book for you is that over the past twenty years, sports psychology has enabled me to become a renowned and internationally recognized coach. Before the age of fifty, I was awarded "The All-Time Great Coach Award" by the sport of volleyball's governing body, USA Volleyball. At first, I thought someone wanted me to retire!

Sports practices driven by psychology have led me to become the all-time winningest coach in the history of Division III Men's Volleyball and enabled my teams to set numerous NCAA records, including, but not limited to eleven National Championships. With all of this experience and success, I came to believe that coaches on all levels could benefit from the education and background in sport psychology that Springfield College had provided for me.

Please understand that I do not diminish the trials and overwhelming challenges that coaching ten-years-old can present. I was truly surprised to find that I was far more tired after running a ninety-minute practice for my son's ten-year-olds soccer team than I was for planning and managing one of my college practice sessions!

Coaching youth sports is a daunting and overwhelming challenge. I will never forget the compliment I was paid by Collin Powers, a past USA Volleyball Pipeline Director, who asked me to coach the youngest age group in the USA Volleyball National Team Pipeline for a few summers. He explained that he believed the best coaches should be at our youngest participation level.

I am proud to say that two players from that group I coached are now National Team participants including Micah Christenson, the starting setter on the United States Bronze Medal Olympic Men's Volleyball team in Rio de Janeiro, Brazil. I am grateful to have had the opportunity to work with these players as young players, and again years later as a consultant coach with our Men's National for the four years leading up to and through the 2016 Olympics.

The youth sport level is the hardest level to coach at because managing this age group takes, not only organization and skill and patience, but a true understanding of the psychological needs of your players. For a variety of reasons children can get off task in a hurry. As well, something that a volunteer youth sport coach might not think about is that coaches are automatically dealing with the mental health of every child on their roster.

Most likely, coaches are graciously willing to sacrifice their time, add direction to the team and spend time with their children but are not prepared to understand how to deal with the coaching techniques required or the psychology of this age group and care for their mental health all at the same time.

Since coaching youth sports is this complicated and important, it is vital that we have fully educated coaches at the earliest levels of competition. That said, we all know that is not generally the case. Most youth sports programs at the local levels depend on the parents who volunteer to coach, but more often than not, they are thrown, or volunteered, into the position with no little or no experience, competency, training, or understanding of sound principles of great coaching.

Some of these "coaches" have little experience in the sport at all. Others may have had some experience participating in sports at some point in their development. However, playing at a Division I school in college or even at the semi or professional sports level, does not necessarily prepare someone for transition to the role of youth sport coach. If we are honest, we will admit that the most inexperienced coaches are assigned to the youngest and least skilled athletes.

Most people who volunteer their time to coach youth sports are altruistically motivated. As coaches, they want to spend time with their kids, give back to their community, or keep alive their own love for sports and competition. They should be commended for wanting to stay involved. Yet their role as a coach is far too important to have them enter this field without sufficient training and education as they are working with children during the most impressionable years of their lives.

This is why I wrote this book: to provide a guide for all youth sport coaches. This book is for you even if you have coached youth sports before or coached an elite or premier youth sport team. This book is for you, even if you have played the sport at a highest level. This book is for you, especially if you have never coached before.

There is a lot to learn and coaching youth sports is more challenging than coaching at the elite levels of a sport. Coaching youth sports is more challenging because it requires more management of the team and the players are less independent in managing themselves. Many youth sport coaches model their own coaching styles after the coaches that they have had or have seen on TV or in the movies. Nothing could be more frightening.

Today, coaching a team with participants from 8–14 years old is a common yet unique experience in America. The hope of this book is to provide you with the direction and a structure that can help you as coaches successfully develop healthy athletes, teammates, and youth sport participants. This book provides a structure to match a variety of goals that all the teammates bring to a season, including competing and developing their skills to adding value and self-improving.

I present the following pages to you with passion. The passion for being the best coach possible and the passion to share a structured approach to coaching that will make the youth sports experience a positive one for all participants. This structure includes all aspects of coaching: communicating with players and team-building; creating warm ups and practice plans; developing all types of players; providing a physically and emotionally safe environment for all participants; and creating competitive strategy. All these factors contribute to the physical and psychological barometer of the team, and will forecast success for the coach.

FOR ALL YOUTH SPORTS COACHES

The coaching structure provided in this book is helpful for all youth sport coaches no matter what the level. Town recreational teams and regional premier elite teams all need to provide an effective structure, one that gives your team the chance to be prepared and to play to their potential. Some part of this book is intended for beginners. Other parts may benefit those who have dabbled in coaching but are now preparing to coach their second or third child's teams. Other parts are for the elite youth sport coaches.

My hope is that there will be something new for everyone, from those who have never played the sport they are coaching to those who have played professionally in the sport they are now instructing. This book will provide an outline of how you can prepare, implement, and evaluate your season and your coaching. I am thrilled to be able to share my structure and passion with you. Go Team!

Acknowledgments

Thank you to all who helped make this book possible. For all my proofreaders including my best proofreader, my wife Maggie, Scott MacGilpin, John LaSpada, Mike Lage and Scott McPhee. Thanks for taking the time to support the book. Since I have met Kevin Sheehan through working on my first book, *Winning the Game of Belief, Cultivating the Cultural Grit that Defines America's Greatest Coaches*, I am grateful for the amazing amount of support he has given me. Kevin was a key contributor in this book and in typical fashion for him he was a consummate giver of his time, energy, and heart. Thanks Kevin.

I have to thank my mother, Mary Elizabeth Sullivan, and my father, Robert E. Sullivan. My Mom was an English teacher for 30+ years. I come from a family of six kids. Mom and Dad required all the kids to spend time writing with Mom. My parents never forced me to fulfill the household writing requirement. They realized I belonged out in the fields and on the courts writing my own future. Ironically, I was moved to write this book. The time to write this book made up for lost time I never spent at the dining room table. Thanks Mom and Dad! I would like to thank my kids who have tolerated me being their coach or videotaping their skill execution in the back yard. The time spend together was valuable and fun. Whether I was coaching you or driving with you to the game and watching, the most important thing for you to know is that I love to watch you play sports!

Thanks to my brother Billy for his contributions and to all my family who supported me in all my athletic endeavors.

It is amazing to think of all the people who have affected my growth as a coach along the way. I have met so many great people through coaching. College Men's Volleyball coaches make up a great group of people and I am proud to be part of such a close, sharing, and fun community of coaches, many of whom are great friends. Meeting all these great people is what it is all about. It would be too difficult to list them so thanks to all the great coaches and friends I have learned from and shared so many great times with over the years.

Introduction

This book will first give you what we know about the youth sport population in America from research. The research gives coaches a chance to know the clientele that make up youth sports. If we know the needs of youth sport participants, we will be better able to provide them with an experience that meets their needs and provides satisfaction.

After getting to know the population we will be coaching, the book provides a step by step process to creating your team's structure. Coaching is creating your own masterpiece. This book will help you build your masterpiece by starting with a solid foundation. It enables a coach to create a skyscraper of success for them and most importantly, for the athletes.

Youth sport has a variety of participants. Every youth sport athlete brings his or her own personality to the team and each person's personality is as unique as their fingerprint. The structure provided in this book will provide instruction on how to get all the personalities on the team progressing in the same direction. This structure serves the needs of those who are really serious about excelling in the sport and those who are involved just to learn and test the waters of their enjoyment.

One question a coach should always be able to answer is "why." Why is it important to plan your practice with so much detail? Why did you choose that drill? Why did you choose that point of emphasis to go with that skill? Why do you count down like that? Why is your practice one hour or two? After reading this book you will have a lot of answers. You will know so much about the craft of coaching and your players will benefit. The decisions and reasons you give in response to the question "why" will be based on science and principles that make the youth sport experience beneficial for everyone including the parents of the children on your teams.

Maybe you coach an outdoor youth sport and the cold or rainy weather is challenging the motivation of your participants. There are methods that you can use that will instantly excite your players and increase their focus on the skills that directly correlate to your team's success. For example, the number one weapon coaches possess to make changes in their players and sell them the product they are delivering is their voices. Many coaches do not realize the importance of every word they chose when addressing the team. This book gives you information that will change your language when coaching young players. Giving feedback is the skill that exposes a coach's inexperience the most.

There are many skills that a teacher uses in the classroom or the gym that are valuable for all coaches. This book outlines teaching methods that are useful to use as coaches. These tricks will work magic with your team, adding to the already effective structure and giving your youth sport participants more comfort in trying new skills, participating without fear of failure, and handling errors as opportunities for growth. A teacher is not so concerned with the scoreboard in their classroom. A teacher is more concerned with their student's growth. Good coaches follow this model and use the methods of a teacher.

Unfortunately, a team's biggest test is game day. Be prepared with great organization but the most important thing a coach must do is be prepared mentally. Competition can lend itself toward a coach losing his or her focus but this book will give coaches methods to enable them to keep their attention in a place that is best for the kids.

There are other youth sport models other than the one we know in America. We can learn from other cultures and their approach to organizing their young athletes. As coaches, we should use anything we can to learn about our perspective and approach to coaching youth sports. We want to make the experience the best possible one for the players.

The youth sports level is arguably the most important level to coach. We know the youth sport level is very difficult to coach at and the leaders need training and education. This age group can lose focus quickly and if you do not set up a great structure, it will happen even quicker than you can imagine. This book will give you methods and serve as your education as to how to be a great youth sport coach.

Overall, the book is designed for you to be the best coach possible by enabling you to create a structure that is safe and comfortable for all different types of participants. After reading this book your structure will give your team the best opportunity to learn and perform. You will have a lot of answers to the question "why" and most importantly, you will be developing life skills for the kids, both on and off the field or court. Many people think that signing their child up for youth sports will automatically offer them the development of life skills. Unfortunately, this is not the case.

This time period is crucial in a child's development. This model of assembling a youth sports team will give you the best chance to offer a team that develops skills and enables your group to perform to their potential, but most importantly gives the participants the platform to develop self-confidence, perseverance, positive social and emotional learning and use strengths to contribute to a team.

This book is gives you the chance to construct a positive environment for the mental health of all youth sport participants. In a comfortable environment for a child, the child would have the opportunity to learn and understand emotions, set and achieve positive goals, feel and show empathy for others, establish and maintain positive relationships, have the opportunity how to make reasonable decisions. A youth sport model such as this will set your players up for future success in life and sports. This would be the ideal environment for all participants.

Every child has their own person growth timeline. This book offers a model that enables a child's timeline to unfold naturally. Youth sports should not force kids to drop out or leave them behind. The youth sport model you present should allow all to benefit and all should have the opportunity to grow and strengthen their physical and mental skills. You should be confident that you are going to be equipped with the skills to be a National Championship Coach after reading this book.

SUMMARY

This book presents a clear structure and mindful approach that any youth sport coach can adopt. The following chapters provide insight on how to lay the foundation for a great season as well as a straight-forward philosophy that will help a coach:

- Develop an understanding of each skill in the sport, how to teach it and refine performance.
- Understand Motor Learning and the science of how kids learn skills the best.
- Create core values that will help athletes choose appropriate behaviors and carry over into life beyond athletics.
- Introduce various teaching styles that are developmentally appropriate for kids of different ages.
- Review the art and science of feedback that helps motivate athletes and individuals.

- Organize activities effectively so the athletes get the most repetitions possible in a short amount of time.
- Learn how to structure a practice with drills and activities that include competition to increase transfer into competition and focus, but are still fun.
- Recognize skills that teachers use that coaches can copy to manage a team.
- Understand how to handle errors and failures.
- Understand how to use competition and goal setting in practice so the players can get the most game like practice in the shortest amount of time
- Steal some tricks that teachers use to be effective at getting their students to learn better.
- Be a good coach during competition. How to organize and where a coach's focus should be on game day.
- Review a sample of youth sports in other countries and what Americans can learn from other models.

These guiding principles will ensure that all youth sports participants are given the opportunity to feel comfortable, competent, and successful so that most importantly, rather than solely focusing on winning, they grow as players and people, and remain excited about playing the next season. Their youth sport experience will give them the ability to improve as a player and learn skills that will assist them in challenging times during their adulthood.

Chapter 1

Youth Sport Research

What We Know about Youth Sports

So now you are a coach. Somehow, you were drafted. After the town league meeting there were more teams than expected and the need for another coach was paramount. Everyone told you it was a cinch and before you knew it, you were given a golf shirt and a whistle. Although you were a bit nervous at the meeting, your friends and neighbors all seemed so confident. How hard could it be? You did play high school basketball after all...

RESEARCH

According to recent studies, as many as 45 million children participate in youth sports in the United States. Sixty-nine percent of girls and 75% of boys participate in some form of organized or team sport. That is an astounding number! When parents register their children for these activities, they do so with the hopes that their children will have a positive experience and be successful. They imagine an activity that involves making new friends, learning cooperation, exploring a new sport, becoming skilled, gaining confidence, getting exercise, and having fun.

Youth sport leagues start as a vehicle to provide an opportunity for children to experience the sport or activity. Unfortunately, as youth sports evolve, many of the reasons parents first got their children involved become overshadowed by a drive to win and become the best in preparation for the next level.

In our world today, many have come to see youth sports as the pipeline to the college of their dreams or a free education. Despite the dreams and promise of youth sports, the sad fact is that the vast majority of those 45 million children will not go on to play sports in high school or beyond. That fact is not just natural attrition, but a direct result of the way that we conduct youth sports in America.

A youth sport environment that is not a safe psychological and emotional place can have lasting and detrimental impact on the developing mind. Consider a preschooler. The mind of a three-year-old is trusting, nonjudgmental, open, curious and learning, and grows at an incredible rate. Studies focused on divergent thinking, or the ability to consider multiple perspectives, are as much as ten times higher in kindergarteners than six graders. And the older the child gets, sadly, characteristics such as creativity and divergent thinking continue to diminish. Unfortunately, youth sports follow a similar trajectory.

Take flag football as an example. Flag football grew out of the anxiety parents and adults had regarding head injuries and the long-term effect of brain trauma. When flag football began as a recreational alternative for kids, it started out with the same creativity that characterizes the mind of a three-year-old. There was minimal adult structure. Kids often made their own plays and followed a simple set of self-enforced rules. Many flag football leagues ran beautifully for a couple of years, until someone decided that the league champion from one town should play the league champion from the next town over.

That is where the problem began and the decline of what had been an experience of pure joy began. Similar to a mind of a three-year-old, the league's effectiveness of serving 90% of its population as a safe place to grow mentally and emotionally diminished. Fast forward ten years when there will be regional, state, and national flag football championships with the promise of college scholarships. Things will look different for those young kids just starting out in the game.

When the coaches are worried about winning more than the development of their participants, there is a problem. When the league focuses on the coaches more than the development of its players the youth sport mission is lost. When a team does not perform well, the coach and parents have come to believe it is really a reflection of the quality of the coaching rather than the ability of players.

Parents are obsessed with the desire that their daughters and sons develop the skills necessary to be able to advance to the next level. Society judges success in athletics, at any level, by wins and losses. On Long Island, there have been situations where teams losing in a county lacrosse final often require police protection from parents when the bus arrives back to the school parking lot.

When my daughter was eight years old, she came home from one of her first soccer games with the biggest smile on her face. She was proudly wearing her team uniform, complete with matching socks and a number on her jersey. As she climbed out of the car, one well-intentioned neighbor yelled across the front lawn, "Did you have a game?" That was a silly question. It was not Halloween. When she replied, "Yes," you can probably guess the neighbor's next question: "Did you win?" And with the simple question, a new line of thinking took place in her young mind.

There was a puzzled look on her face. After that question she reflected on her game through a whole new lens. With that one question, my neighbor had started to change her whole reason for playing. Originally after her first game in the car ride home, the only thing she was trying to figure out was how could the coaches expected her to run again after eating the most delicious orange slices at halftime. It wasn't long before she changed activities.

What We Know *about* Young Athletes

We know that 45 million youth sport participants are "intensely" involved in a wide range of activities. Youth sports participants can spend up to twenty hours a week in that particular sport starting at age five or six. In addition, many sports today are often played year-round rather than during just one season or a few months a year. If a young athlete is interested in exploring more than one sport, the number of hours a week they are playing organized sports can easily double or triple. This intense participation can put school on the back burner for ambitious athletes.

This participation equates to greater commitment and becomes increasingly important, not only to the participants but also to the coaches and parents. Many parents worry about this intensity, but feel intense pressure that if they do not succumb, their child will be disadvantaged in some way, or left behind. Parents and young athletes often find themselves on a treadmill that they cannot get off of.

The "youth" in youth sports is roughly defined as ages 8–14, but in some cases can start as young as three years old. Developmental psychology maintains these same years as critical periods of development for self-esteem, personality, drive, and compassion. Parents believe participation in organized sports can teach their kids "important life lessons." However, participation does not always equate to an automatic acquisition of these benefits and can lead to quite the opposite result.

Children will only be able to develop these characteristics if the environment is safe and structured to provide these growth opportunities. Most of us can most likely remember a great teacher or coach from your childhood, but you may just as easily recall a teacher or coach that was negative or abusive. In fact, as humans, we often tend to focus on the negative more than the positive. These impressions, whether positive or negative, can be long lasting and even permanent.

In order for a youth sport program to benefit all participants, it must have competent coaches. This is why the most important implications of sport psychology are focused on youth sports. Good coaches rarely take over a team and implement a system. Good coaches, first need to go through a "listen and learn" period.

After a period of conscientious and intentional observation, the coach can gauge the barometer of what is needed for the team and program and begin to develop a system or structure that would be good to put in place. One size does not fit all. The real motivation for this book is that now that you are assigned role of coach, does not mean that you are ready to assume that role.

How many youth sport coaches have an idea of what is important to the children at the developmental level that they are at? How many coaches realize that one team of ten-year old players is totally different than another team of ten-year-old participants? Children participate in sports to have fun. That is the number one reason at all levels.

Not just joking around, but fun. Although peer relationships through sports are important to kids, and fun, it is also "fun" to learn new skills, work at something challenging, compete against yourself and others, be a part of something bigger than yourself, a team, and to develop and enhance your individual fitness. Having success at anything is fun and fun is more than laughing with friends. Self-actualization is the ultimate fun.

Participation in youth sports can also help young athletes develop self-confidence, self-esteem, and efficacy during a crucial time period. The youth sport experience can provide the opportunity to experience all of the fun team rituals including participating in tournaments, hearing parents cheer from the sidelines, participating in a well-organized practice, receiving positive feedback from coaches, and working hard.

Some of these aspects are more enjoyable for certain players than others. Girls and boys will prioritize this list differently. That is why it is important for youth sport leaders to understand why kids play sports in the first place and to adapt their practices to the needs of their athletes.

One of the saddest trends in youth sports today is the number of children dropping out of organized play. Some of the most common reasons kids give for withdrawing from youth sports are not having fun, not being "good enough" to play, and not liking the coach. Sound coaching development systems can prevent participants from feeling this way. A good system considers the motives and strengths of the group and forms a structure around those characteristics. This is why it is so important that youth sport coaches are taught how to structure a system that makes the sport fun for kids to learn, develop, and compete. A system highlights kid's strength rather than implicitly or explicitly tells kids that they are not good enough. Not easy, but obtainable.

Out of the 45 million, 30% will drop the sport before the next season begins. According to National Alliance for Youth Sports, 75% of kids in the U.S. stop playing organized sports by the age of 13. One measurement to evaluate the success of a youth sport season is not the number of wins and losses, but rather how many participants return to play again next season.

Maybe you have witnessed a child who had a great experience one year and was beyond excited for the next season to begin, only to be let down due to the fact the next environment does not match their interest and the structure is not as effective. Thirty percent equates to losing over 13,000,000 players a season. This number is alarming and undoubtedly impacts the lives of children across America.

PERCEIVED COMPETENCE

Some youth sport coaches will have a group of players assigned to them. Even in a youth sport league that includes a draft, coaches will end up having players assigned to them that they might not ever choose. Everyone can sign up if they can pay, and especially if they can donate time or additional funds.

An uneducated coach may assume that there is nothing they can do with this athlete who is not comparable in skill level to the other players. This undrafted player could also not share the same enthusiasm as the others. Contrary to that thinking, the development of this player should be the number one goal of youth sport coaches, even if the coach would describe him or herself as a very competitive person. Most coaches do not have the skill set, nor the motivation to take on that challenge. But the development of this player is a vital, but often ignored role of the youth coach.

Perceived competence is an essential component of youth sports. Perceived competence on the part of the player determines, not only if a participant will continue in an activity, but if he or she will even join in the first place. One of the coach's most important roles is to help the players build their perceived competence. This perception can lead to developing self-esteem and social skills that will equip this young person for life beyond athletics. Many coaches are not prepared for this role, and the additional burden of adjusting to the unique personality and talents of each individual player. The good news is, with appropriate education and attention, coaches can learn how to make the most of this role.

One thing that a coach can do to help improve a child's perceived competence is to find what the child is good at, improve that skill so the team can utilize that skill or talent. Using a strengths-based approach with an individual enhances his or her overall well-being and allows the player to feel like an active participant. Most coaches want to help all kids improve, so they may mistakenly focus on correcting the players' weaknesses. However, too much focus on improving the weaknesses misses the opportunity to build on strengths, especially when, in a short youth sport season, some weaknesses may not improve regardless. The idea of a strengths approach is often missed by coaches at all levels, but can be learned with an increased focus.

Who is to really say that a child is not good enough? It may appear to be obvious who should play to win-driven coaches, but all children also deserve respect and trust. Unfortunately, by the time children are old enough to participate on organized sports teams, they have become very good at quickly figuring out who is "good" and who is not. Often, these perceptions are based on what they see and hear from other players, parents, and coaches. Coaches, intentionally or not, tend to focus most of their time and attention on the "best" players. However, all players need to feel like they can contribute in some meaningful way. This is where the expert training of the coach comes into play.

In most youth sport rosters there are the most skilled three and least skilled three participants. The irony of coaching the least three skilled is important not only to build their self-esteem but also for the team's overall level of play. Many coaches would think that focusing more on the "big three" would be best for the team but giving more time and confidence to the least-skilled three would help the team be more successful. A strategy most youth sport coaches do not implement.

An effective way to build perceived competence in all is to evaluate all participants against themselves rather than each other. If the child is primarily concerned about being the best on the team, they will not have the persistence to survive the rigor of youth sports. Instead, if the participants are focused on improving their own skills and contributing in their own unique way, we may be able to develop a passion and persistence which will enable them to grow. It can be difficult to make this a priority when philosophically, winning is often the most important thing for youth coaches and parents.

Let's keep in my mind, what a successful youth sport season should look like. While wins and losses are important, a far more significant indicator of success should be how many players have a comfortable level of perceived competence and how many are willing and excited to come back and participate again next season.

SPECIALIZATION AND ANXIETY LEAD TO AN INCREASE IN INJURIES

Youth sport injuries are more common today more than ever. Young athletes have always been prone to the occasional broken bone or sprained ankle injuries, but we know today it is increasingly common for youth sport participants to experience ACL tears, rotator cuff and labrum surgeries, concussions, and stress fractures. Reports indicate that these increases in traumatic injuries in youth sports are often the result of kid's specialization or choosing one sport that is played year-round. Specialization prevents a young body from resting certain muscle groups and leads to overuse. In addition, it prevents children from developing all of the different muscle groups in their growing bodies.

Playing a variety of sports that require a different set of muscles helps prevent overuse injuries. We know that children are sustaining more serious injuries at a higher rate due to a schedule that involves participating in multiple sports at one time and not implementing activities that are low impact or nonstressful. Also, athletes are starting their careers earlier, sometimes as young as the age of four. When activity becomes too intense over a short period of time, or is not developmentally appropriate for the growing body, the overuse injuries that were usually reserved for adult participants begin to occur in higher frequency in youth sport participants.

When a youth sport environment increases in physical intensity, it also adds anxiety. Sport psychologists know that an increase in anxiety increases the probability of sport injuries. When you play on an "elite" youth sport team, it is understood that the training will be more frequent, and intense. As this intensity increases, so can the pressure and anxiety the child feels. Elite teams also typically train year-round as the athletes' bodies are changing and growing. Overuse during these growth periods can be dangerous for young participants.

In addition, the concentrating on one sport at the expense of all others, limits the carry over and transfer of skills from one sport to another that may actually enhance performance in the athlete's chosen sports. For instance, the physical demands of football may actually better prepare the lacrosse player for the physical demands of lacrosse than playing lacrosse all year-round. Research and statistics bear out the fact that athletes that have developed to the highest levels of their sport have had a broad and rich background as young athletes.

David Epstein's book, *Range: Why Generalists Triumph in a Specialized World,* challenges the deliberate practice doctrine of grit and specialization suggests that engaging in a broad range of activities leads to greater success in both athletics and life. The research driving Epstein's work provides strong evidence that having your child abandon all other sports and focus on one sport may be the worst thing that you could do for a young athlete.

LONG-TERM IMPACTS

Recent studies show that only eight million of the forty-five million kids who participate in youth sports go on to play in high school. Then, only 7% of high school athletes continue to play a varsity sport in college. These are generally the most physical, athletic, and dedicated players in their sports. One would assume they were best served by their youth sports experiences as they have been able to develop into college-ready athletes. Yet, college coaches frequently see the negative effects of youth sports on their athletes.

One would assume that a college athlete would peak during their senior year. Parents and players alike assume this is automatic and with good reason. These players have had the most training. If they have been one of the better performers on their teams, they would have had the most experience in competitions. If their team has won some championships, they should know how to win. Unfortunately, this is not always the case.

One major contributing factor to these athletes fizzling during what should be the peak of their athletic careers is *burn out*. Part of this burn out is due to the fact that these athletes were intensely involved in their sport from a very young age. By the time they are finally mentally and physically most prepared to excel at their sport, they have lost interest or the drive to compete. The experience has just gotten old for them.

Take, for example, the many basketball players who spend a postgraduate year after high school to improve their recruiting opportunities. This intense specialization is often needed to play college sports, even at the NCAA Division III level. Most would think the postgraduate year is only necessary for the highest level of college athletics, but that is not the case. If we start the timeline of "intense" participation in a sport at five or six years old, that continues through middle and high school to a postgraduate year, a red shirt year in college, and four more years of college play, there have been literally countless hours spent training at the highest level, and all of this time and experience can take a toll on these athletes.

Staying with basketball, you could imagine that dedicating all those years to playing and playing year-round in the best AAU tournaments all through the summer and competing for a National Championship starting in third grade would be worth it if you are the first player drafted in the NBA draft. However, if you are that Division III student athlete who is playing for the love of the game, you can see by your senior year how these athletes are fatigued and burnout is likely.

In this scenario, youth sports become the foundation for everything. It is the foundation for building mental health, fundamental skills, strategic understanding, efficiency, focus, and drive. In many ways, participation in youth sports is a long-term experiment with the end result only becoming evident when the young participants finally become adults. Youth sport coaches must remember that they have the unique opportunity to "have fun" with this process and make it enjoyable for all participants.

Sometimes, the best performer at age twelve receives unintentional yet damaging feedback that comes naturally as a result of their success. These athletes might think of their success as a result of their inborn talent. They often hear that they are more athletic or just "really good" at their game. As a result, these athletes do not equate their success with their effort and process, which will only become detrimental as time goes on and the competition increases.

The best young athletes need coaching and direction to buy into the growth mindset that Carol Dweck explains in her book, *Mindset: The New Psychology of Success*. Attributing success to things within one's control, such as effort and attitude, generally do not emerge naturally out of the typical youth sports environment. But a strong coach can work to provide a system that will help each player develop to his or her highest potential.

It is also critical to remember that losing is an important part of the process. Too much focus on the nine-year-old championship is not the best thing. Falling short in that championship game might be the best thing to happen in terms of the overall growth and development of any individual player. The story of Michael Jordan not making his high school varsity basketball team yet going on to become one of the greatest players of all time is a perfect example.

Of course, it's not always easy to remember this when at that nine-year-old championship game, there are five times more fans than a regular season game, the coach has expressed his or her desperate desire to win, the league now has assigned four officials instead of two, and in some cases, the competition, may be aired on local television. All this makes it difficult to believe that being the best and winning are not the most important parts of the game. This is why the coach's role in youth sports is vital.

The best performer at twelve years old may receive damaging feedback that comes naturally as a result of their success. They could think of their success as a result of their innate ability. This is more common than that athlete believing they were successful because of their effort and process. The best young athletes need coaching and direction to buy into the growth mindset that Carol Dweck explains to us in her book, *Mindset: The New Psychology of Success*. Attributing success to controllable items, like effort and attitude do not come naturally out of the typical youth sport environment. All the reason for a coach to have a great system in place.

SUMMARY

Clearly, youth sports touch the lives of millions of children each year, and these experiences can have lasting impacts on the physical, emotional, and mental health of the participants. The goal of parents, coaches, players, and all involved is that youth sports will provide a positive experience from which all children will benefit. But we also know that this is not always the case. Factors such as misguided priorities, lacking an educational structure, the unique needs and strengths of children of different ages can all present challenges to a successful experience.

Self-confidence, the children's priority to have fun, and understanding why most kids drop out of youth sports are not the typical agenda items on the first meeting with the parents in a youth sport season. In order to be truly successful, coaches who have most likely just signed up to help out with the team and spend some extra time with their own kids will have to battle the mentality of children that is formed naturally from the automatic feedback that they receive from society, such as the neighbor, or parent, wanting to know if they won or how many they scored in the game.

Trying to help a lesser performing player to perceive his or her own competence as important and contributing is not easy. In fact, not many aspects of coaching at the youth sport level can be more demanding. This challenge will require greater effort and insight than coaching at the elite level.

We know that it is difficult to convince parents and others that increasing specialization and intensity at a young age is rarely beneficial for children's long-term development. Too many parents have unrealistic dreams of college scholarships dancing in their heads. We know that burnout is a real factor in the college age and we are even now seeing it in high school age players. We know that the increase in the number and severity of injuries at the youth sport level is real, and that some of these injuries can be career ending, even as early as twelve in some athletes.

This book presents a clear structure and mindful approach that any youth sport coach can adopt. The following chapters provide insight on how to lay the foundation for a great season as well as a straight-forward philosophy that will help a coach:

- Develop an understanding of each skill in the sport, how to teach it and refine performance.
- Understand Motor Learning and the science of how kids learn skills the best.
- Core values that will help athletes choose appropriate behaviors and carry over into life beyond athletics.

- Introduce various teaching styles that are developmentally appropriate for kids of different ages.
- Review the art and science of feedback that helps motivate athletes and individuals.
- Understand how to organize activities so the athletes get the most repetitions possible in a short amount of time.
- Learn how to structure a practice with drills and activities that include competition to increase transfer into competition and focus, but are still fun.
- Recognize skills that teachers use that coaches can copy to manage a team.
- How to handle errors and failures.
- implementing goal setting so the players can get the most game like practice in the shortest amount of time

These guiding principles will ensure that all youth sports participants are given the opportunity to feel comfortable, competent, and successful, so that most importantly, rather than solely focusing on winning, they grow as players, and people, and remain excited about playing the next season and will even carry their learning into adulthood.

Chapter 2

How to Structure Your Team

Methods to Set Your Team Up for Success

PLANNING BEFORE FIRST PRACTICE

Before the first practice begins, coaches have a great deal of work to do. If you know who all the coaches are before the first practice, you are fortunate and should take advantage of your time to get organized. Sometimes, the head coach meets the assistant coaches at the first practice. If this is the case, then the head coach should have already done some major organizational work and should plan on meeting shortly before practice to review roles for day one. There should be an agreement to meet again before the second practice and to continue to review the structure of the team with everyone involved. Here are some things that a coaching staff should have completed before the first practice.

TEACHING CUES—FUNDAMENTAL RESEARCH

Coaches need to speak the same language to the players. To accomplish this, the head coach should take the time to research the skills of the sport including the best cues to use to teach each skill. When the coaches decide on the best cues, they should use those cues consistently with the players. One coach should not teach the skills differently than the rest of the coaches. Even if you think you are an expert on the sport or skills, take the time to look around and compare what you find to what you already know. This will either lead to new information or validate what you already know.

    A teaching cue is a short phrase that gives the learner something to focus on to perform the skill efficiently. The cue identifies crucial elements of the motor skill. By focusing on the cue, the performer builds an effective movement pattern in the brain. The more an athlete focuses on the cue during practice, the more automatic these skills become during competition. The best cues are short, memorable, even a little funny, and cover several movements.

Cues change based on the age group that you work with. It is very important that coaches chose cues that are developmentally appropriate and correct for the age group. The same axiom applies for activities. If the cues and the activities are not appropriate for the age group, the participants will get easily frustrated. Be sure to research cues that are developmentally appropriate for the age group of the sport participants.

So, what does a good teaching cue look like in practice? An effective cue to teach kids, or anyone, to throw is, "Show off all of your arm pit." Many times, a coach may direct a young player to "keep their elbow above the shoulder" or "pull your arm all the way back." The problem with these cues is that the player may not be able to visualize or feel these cues.

Effective teaching cues are ones that all players, regardless of athletic ability, can easily access. Also, a good cue gets all the movement necessary for success in a short, understandable phrase or sentence. "Show me more of that arm pit," gets the thrower to pull their arm all the way back and gets the elbow high above the shoulder at the same time.

Asking a young thrower to "show off all of your arm pit" is something they can do very easily. You can even make a joke of it to increase the chances of the players remembering it. "Arm pits have a bad reputation but, on this team, we love to show off our arm pits." The great cues become something that players share with their parents on the way home. "Hey Mom, coach said he really loves my arm pit." Once you identify a good teaching cue, be sure all of the coaches use the same words as they teach the skill.

For each skill, you should limit the number of cues to three to five. Too many cues become difficult for the learner and their effectiveness is lessened. Sometimes as the season progresses and you feel that a skill is not developing, you might want to recreate the cues for that skill. In this case, work with the other coaches on your team and agree upon revised cues that emphasize a new movement pattern. You can even explain to the players why you are changing the cues for the skill, as young players may be more likely to engage if they understand the why.

Additionally, although you may identify several teaching cues for one skill, some players may need to tackle them one at a time. This poses a challenge because it is tempting to address all of the motions or cues that the player is struggling with at the same time. Resist the temptation. Especially with a struggling or novice player, it is critical that you focus on one cue at a time to keep the athlete's focus on that one aspect of the skill.

This is best taught in station work. For example, create five stations, one for each cue, and the athletes can progress through the stations, performing the same skill while focusing on one cue at a time. If you are unsure about what cue to teach first, start with the beginning phase of the skill, such as the ready position. John Wooden's first practice started with teaching players to properly tie their shoes. Don't be afraid to stress the basics.

Lastly, current research shows that external cues are more effective than internal cues. An internal cue for the arm swing in the running motion is "swing your hand back behind your body." Just dealing with the body relative to where their hand is, performers, especially young ones, might have difficulty really feeling this cue.

An external cue has nothing to do with the body. The same cue is made an external cue by saying, "pretend you had a handful of spaghetti in your hand and you are throwing it as far as you can behind you every time you swing your arm back." The cue is then simplified to, "Throw that spaghetti." Hopefully, even an eight year-old player will ask you, "Cooked or not cooked?" This enables you to make a joke and make the cue more memorable. The athlete processes the external cue better than the cue that deals with body position.

Here are some examples of cues that I have used for 10–12-year-old baseball players.

Batting Cues

1. Loaded balance—"Be athletic"
2. Hands at Ear—"Listen to the Sea Shell"
3. Hands stay above the ball—chop down at ball—bottom of bat at ball—"Stay on top of the ball
4. Late step—"Wait and step"
5. Middle of the ball—"Knock the dishes off the table" (Follow through)
6. Line drives the key—"Get some Lasers Beams"

Throwing Cues

1. Get feet in position to throw—"Feet set"—(even when rushing)
2. Prepare to throw—Get "Set up" ball to ear
3. Throwing motion—"Show off your arm pit"
4. Step toward target—"Feet step to where you are throwing"
5. Follow through—Have your "fingers follow the ball"

Ground Balls Cues

1. Ready position—"Get glove dirty"

2. Shuffle in front of the ball—"Chin stays low"—Make the movement a "Tik Tok dance"
3. Two hands—"Double avoids trouble"
4. 2 or 3 steps toward first base—"Feet guide the ball"

CORE VALUES

One of the most revered core values of the military is "No Man or Woman left behind." It is hard to imagine when you are watching one of those special operation military movies that a group of eight soldiers, upon realizing that one of their peers got shot behind enemy lines, would go back to get them, facing up to five hundred enemy soldiers. It would be hard to imagine that these soldiers would risk their lives unless you realize how driven and defined the military are by their core values.

Not only do military personnel follow the core values, they live them. The military personnel understand, believe, and are dedicated to the core values. This makes the decision to go back into enemy territory, not only possible, but the only course of action that they will consider. They are committed to behaviors defined by their internal core value, "No man or woman left behind."

Core values help members of the team make decisions in all aspects of life but especially in critical situations. When the players follow the core values of a team, their behaviors and decisions for any situation are clear and indisputable. It is important to establish core values with your team so the players can make the decisions the coach feels are important in creating a team culture. Here is a sample of core values for a 12-year-old baseball team. Although this example is derived for a 12-year-old baseball team, these Core Values are completely transferable to any age group or youth sport.

CORE VALUES—12-year-old baseball team

1. Work hard and play to your potential every pitch.
2. Keep a positive attitude about your ability especially when you experience failure. (Example, strikeouts, errors, walks. No one is perfect. This is what being good at baseball is about. *Use Your Reset Button—like a computer!*) Believe.
3. Communicate positively with your teammates—both verbal and body language.
4. Focus on fundamentals coaches are sharing with you.
5. Focus on playing your best inning and do not talk about winning or losing the game.

These core values should be the first thing introduced on the very first day of practice. They are the most important lessons the coaches will share that season. Create a chart or sign listing these core values and post them on a neon pink poster board at every practice and game. Make a copy of the core values and send one home with each player. When a player is off task, refer to the core value that should strive to perform better.

For example, a player might be showing negative body language and frustration when a teammate made an error. That player would then be informed that they were not doing well with core value number three and were asked to review the core value and make sure he or she understood the core value before they came out. Emphasize the importance of being positive with teammates at all times so the team could work better together.

Some of your core values may be difficult for an eleven-year-old. However, it is part of your job as a coach to establish the ground rules. The team's core values are the foundation for the team's success. They will create a safe and healthy environment for all to succeed, regardless of skill level. Core value number two provides a guide for players to handle the pressure. The reset button is like an imaginary button on their heads that they can push in the same way they would push the power button to reboot their computer.

Core value number five is so challenging and the team may need to be reminded as a group and as individuals how important it is to be in the present with their focus and how to be their best in that moment. Young players need to be reminded over and over again to focus on the present rather than the past, whether it be a success or failure in a previous game or even a previous play within the game they are playing. Focus on what you can achieve in the present moment is one that many adults are continuously working on. This makes it an especially valuable skill to introduce to children through their participation in youth sports.

Core values are essential to shape your team and they serve as the guiding force, prioritizing which behaviors and attitudes are most important. One way to reinforce these values is to award a "dude" or "dudette" of the day by acknowledging the player who best exemplified the core values during that session. Giving examples of how the core values were carried out is a great way to give positive feedback and encourage players to behave accordingly. It also helps everyone on the team feel good, knowing that the environment has solid structure and is safe.

How many practices have you heard end with what needs to be better? Coaches are constantly demanding more focus, energy, and work ethic and can become easily frustrated with the performance of the team as it reflects poorly on themselves. Therefore, these coaches take out their frustration with themselves on the young players which increases anxiety and decreases the joy and fun for all involved. Dr. Mimi Murray, esteemed Professor of Sports

Psychology at Springfield College, often reminds coaches, "Why not tell your team they are great?" Sadly, this is something many coaches at all levels fail to do, especially after their players experience a loss.

Another powerful tip when creating your core values is to create an "Action Plan." The action plan is something that gives players a concrete description of what it looks like when the team is following the core values and performing to their potential.

Remember, to define success, not defined by wins and losses, but rather by adherence to the team's core values. Here is an example of my Springfield College Men's Volleyball Team's Core Values and Action Plan.

Core Values—Springfield College Men's Volleyball

1. Work hard to win every rally
2. Have your actions enhance our team cohesion
3. Stay in the system by using humanics as a benchmark for your behavior
4. Build relationships by communicating and listening
5. Have a learning mindset
6. Be process oriented
7. Compete every day making yourself and others better
8. Stay connected to the fundamentals you need to improve

Humanics, highlighted in item number 3, is a term that we use at Springfield College to define our mission of treating other people well. Your team could use the strong points of your organization's or your own personal philosophy. This philosophy will guide both the coaches' and the players' decision making. If your philosophy as a basketball coach is that a fast break offense is the best way to score the most points possible, your players do not have to decide what to do with the ball when they rebound. They will push the ball up the floor as fast as possible. Here is our action plan that describes our performance when our players follow our core values . . .

Springfield College Men's Volleyball Action Plan

- FAST—Dominating
- EFFICIENT—Statistically great
- GREAT COMMUNICATION—Body language / mouth & eyes
- SOUND—Great skills
- BELIEF—100% available and 100% ours

When the entire team follows the core values this is the result in our level of play. We play fast and dominate. Our play is efficient. We have goals for each statistic in the game. We know when we achieve these statistical goals our chances of winning increase. When players internalize the core values, they effectively communicate with their words and body language. We display great fundamentals and as a result of all of this we believe we can win. Creating core values and sharing an action plan allows coaches to shape the behaviors they like for your team during the season.

THE COACH'S ROLE

Although every sport is different, they all have various coaching tasks that are necessary. Each coach on any given team should have a very clear role. For example, a basketball team could have a coach who teaches defense, a coach who teaches offense, and a coach responsible for out of bound plays. It is not to say that those coaches are solely responsible for those areas, but they would be the coach who focuses on teaching the kids that part of the game. This makes it easier for the players to know who to rely on for various parts of the game.

A coach should also have designated roles for everything that goes on game day. A big part of youth sports is managing the roster during competitions. Again, all coaches would have the opportunity to give input but one would be assigned to carry out the task. This clear, organized structure gives the kids comfort and belief that they are in a well-run environment. It helps them play to their potential. This also makes practice planning go more smoothly.

COACH'S COMMUNICATION TO THE PARENTS

How a coach communicates with parents is an important yet often overlooked aspect of coaching when one takes on the job. It is so important that there is more information in following chapters. This section simply acknowledges the fact that most coaches need to communicate with parents with some regularity just to share logistical information. For regular email contact, remember these key guidelines: communicate with parents as quickly as possible; keep your emails short and simple; only provide information parents need to be organized.

You can introduce yourself in the first email, but your first and all emails following should be simple with the information of what time to arrive, where to be, what to bring is important. Send this email as soon as you can. If you are coaching an outdoor sport, let parents know about cancellations and how you will proceed with league policies. Stress the importance of being on time and make sure to be 10–15 minutes early yourself. Running a well-organized, planned practice is challenging when some team members arrive late. A head coach needs to be very organized and timely when communicating important information to parents as it establishes a tone and expectation for the season.

SUMMARY

- Coaches need to organize before the first practice. Every practice will affect your team and a lack of organization in the first practice will leave a negative impact on your team.
- Research the fundamentals of your sport and develop the cues the coaches are going to use to teach the skills. All the coaches should say the same thing when coaching.
- Spend time creating cues that are external, memorable, and solve a lot of problems.
- Develop core values to share with your team to help shape desired behaviors. Share and emphasize the core values with your team daily. Help sell the core values with an action plan that depicts what your team looks like when you play to your potential by following the team's core values.
- Define each coach's role including choosing one who will be communicating with the parents.

Chapter 3

Winning Is Important, But . . .

Channeling Your Team's Focus to Play at Their Best

PROCESS VS. PRODUCT ORIENTATION

Winning has a powerful impact on youth sports and not winning or losing is equally as impactful. Remembering from previous chapters that winning is clearly not the number one reason boys or girls play youth sports, but winning or losing effects the whole mood of the team and the impact of the coach. Clearly, winning is on the front of everyone's minds in any youth sport team.

The relationship that a coach has with winning is very counterintuitive. Typically, the more the coach emphasizes winning and talks about the importance of winning, the less successful the participants are in regard to winning. Focusing solely on winning often has the effect of moving individuals farther away from their potential, especially in highly competitive situations. The less the coach emphasizes winning, and the more the coach emphasizes effort and attitude toward their processes, including the team's core values, the more likely it will be that the team wins.

This is a really hard concept for most youth sport coaches to embrace. Too many coaches put real emphasis on post season single elimination pregame speeches that remind the participants that losing will end their season. These, Knute Rockne, dramatic do-or-die speeches, will rarely result in the team playing their best. The added pressure usually ends with the best players on the team having an off game and results in tears from the players during the game-ending team handshakes.

Youth sport coaches who want to move up in the club to coach older or more talented teams feel a real pressure to prove themselves worthy by winning at the younger level. The pressure the coach feels to win is directly translated over to the players. The players feel the stress the coach feels and the need to win can blur what they need to do to win.

Just watch the body language of a youth sport coach during a championship. The youth sport coach who feels the pressure to win will react to every play and every call by the official. If you see a coach wildly celebrating the good plays and showing frustration after the errors, you are probably watching a coach who is experiencing an increased pressure to win.

Coaches who are coaching the players to play their best and who do not feel how well their team played is defined by the win or the loss will exhibit a more consistent body language. For instance, Brad Stevens, the ex-coach of the Celtics, remains in character and does not act like a fan, even when his team hits a buzzer beater to win a game.

Brad Stevens acts like the same coach, no matter how his team is performing or what the score is at the time. There have been interviews when he has been asked about his amazingly calm demeanor after his team has won a game on a buzzer beater. His response embraces a wisdom and a knowledge that should characterize youth coaches. Refusing to define his team's performance on one play, Brad will often state, "that one shot was not going to change whether or not my team played well tonight."

Coaches can often feel as if they have more on the line than the participants. If these kids are mistakenly equating their self-worth and value to the team's success, unfortunately, all too often, so are the coaches. When a team starts to lose more than win, it can be a challenging time for all. Add the fact that the coach may be in over his or her head in regards to organization, management of practices, strategy, teaching effectiveness, competition, and communication, and you can arrive at a point, where coaches are extremely frustrated. Unfortunately, the people who suffer the most in these situations, are the people with the most to lose, the youth players.

The reason why this book is essential for youth sport coaches, even those who have already had a coaching experience, is that this intense focus on winning will undermine every effort to create a successful experience for the players. Even high school coaches need to put a structure in place that will set a team and the participants up for success that is focused on improvement and not solely on winning.

A youth sport leader who creates an effective environment who is a good teacher, usually wins. A team environment that is structured with the organization that this book provides, incorporating the notion that winning is of secondary importance is more likely to win than the coach who stresses a win-at-all cost philosophy. The execution of the team's play and strategies is the only pathway that leads to winning. Ironically, if a coach ignores winning and takes care of all the processes, winning results naturally.

When you effectively structure your youth sport team, you perform like a great coach. This is what leads to winning, rather than an unyielding focus of winning. As an organized coach, kids will believe what you are preaching, and the result will be that your team starts to win. At this point, because of your organization, the increased success of your players will result in even more buy into what you are saying. The result of your increased organization and focus on improvement will make you even more impactful on your team members!

When your team has the correct focus and your team starts winning, your kids will listen to you more. The players will believe more and trust more the things you are saying to them. As a coach, when you perform well in all the areas that this book presents, (core values, organizing coaches, creating an environment that all participants feel safe in, present good cues, run organized practices, feedback really well), your team will perform well and your kids will be aware of your effectiveness as a coach.

The players will notice how effective your strategies and practices are. There are no secrets from players. They are watching your every move and are more insightful than we often realize. The players on your team are excited to learn from you and do not need the increased pressure from the focus to win over the focus to perform. At that point, you can really build your player's belief in their own abilities. As you keep teaching and your players improve, they will perform better and win more. The more effective you are as a coach, the more your players will buy into what you are preaching and the more positive impact you will have on the players.

One of the most important things a youth sport coach can do is define *winning*. What is a win? What does it mean for a team to be successful? John Wooden, the UCLA men's basketball coach, regarded as the ultimate teacher/coach, considered himself a teacher first and a coach second. Wooden has been quoted as saying that during the team's streak of winning ten NCAA Division I National Championships in twelve years, that he never talked about winning or losing a basketball game in any of those years.

Coach Wooden, the absolute winningest coach of all time in men's college Division I basketball, never talked about winning! Does that mean that Coach Wooden wasn't competitive? What did Coach Wooden talk about in place of winning? The "process."

Coach Wooden emphasized a process that defined what was important for the players to focus on. You better believe Coach Wooden was competitive and his most competitive edge was ensuring that the structure he created around his team was solid and everything he did as a coach, supported that structure and gave the players the best chance to play to their potential.

An effective youth sport coach will define a win as controlling all the things that the team can control. The controllable things in sports are the behaviors of the players. The most important thing the players can control is how positive and confident they are they can perform to their potential. To do their best.

The ability for a player to believe they can do their best comes from an ability to control their process of effort, staying positive, being comfortable and secure with themselves, having a great attitude, and communicating well. When a coach focuses on these processes and lets go of the worry about controlling winning or losing these things happen. Ironically, letting go of winning, usually results in the team winning more. The effective youth coach believes and communicates that the "process" is more important the "product."

Winning, or the "product," is most often out of a team's or a coach's control. The official can make a bad call, the weather can be extreme and take away a team's advantage instantly. In a sport like tennis or volleyball, the ball can land an inch out. The player performed beautifully and just missed the line. An error that can be regarded as a good error, but unfortunately, can lead to the loss. By focusing on the product, the coach can be setting their team up for failure. Defining the win as winning the process, rather than the outcome of the game, can guarantee a win, no matter what the score.

Really, if a coach or player is going to show any frustration or anger it should be in regard to their process. If a result is not to their potential and they are not happy with it they should never be upset about the result. Instead they should evaluate how they could have performed better in the process of being confident, relaxed, and not worried about the result to have eliminated any possible distractions. Anger or frustration should only come as a result of realizing the performer chose to think about the things that are only going to take away effort to be their best in that particular moment, the result.

When coaches emphasize the process, they give their team a chance to win, no matter what the score. This is such a good deal for everyone involved. By defining winning as executing the processes a team can control, can always result in a win. We like to share the idea that winning is similar to the farmer who grows the best fruit trees. To grow the best trees, the farmer has to give all of his or her attention to the roots. The great farmer will enjoy the fruit for a moment, but not for long because that will take focus and attention away from the roots.

Another example of paying attention to the most important part of your team is the story behind bamboo wood. Bamboo is the strongest wood that we know of. In addition to being strong, bamboo wood is the lightest. This powerful wood is grown differently than timber or maple wood. You have to plant the seed and take care of the roots for three years, before the bamboo wood sprouts. When growing the strongest wood in the world, the only way to do that is to give all your attention to the roots, for three years.

That is the attention a youth sport coach needs to give to their team's process. A coach that spends all the time he or she has watering the roots of their team will in turn be developing a team that is great at the process. As a result of not focusing on winning, the team will be strong like bamboo and win a lot more games. John Wooden eliminated the distractions that a product orientation can give your team. Coach Wooden focused on the roots and all the processes that his team could control, totally ignoring the ones that he could not control.

Even during practice, a coach that is worried about winning more than improving will get frustrated with a player who makes a lot of errors. This shallow approach will limit the growth opportunities for the player and damage the player's self-efficacy or confidence. Neurologically, it is impossible for a player to learn the motor development movement patterns of a skill without making an error. You don't know what sweet tastes like until you have tasted sour. You cannot often learn to perform a skill properly without first experiencing doing the skill improperly.

How is a youth sport participant, where skill development is crucial to their long-term participation, supposed to learn if they do not feel comfortable making an error? If a player develops a bad habit or fundamental flaw in a skill, they may be able to still dominate based on their physicality but at the higher level, when all the participants are as physically gifted, they are going to fail for the first time and the anxiety they feel at that awkward moment will be debilitating. Better for players to fail early and often.

Failing is great fertilizer for success. Learning how to fail early, not give up, and to persevere when things are difficult is the great life lesson in youth sports. If the environment that the participant is participating in at ten years old is a safe environment, that focused on the process, that player will feel more comfortable and have the freedom to experience failure, and all of its benefits. For teams that are "product orientated" and focus on solely winning, errors will receive feedback and add stress to the developing player.

In addition, efforts that are fundamentally incorrect, but still get a positive result because that player is more mature than most, will get rewarded because of the result. This player will not be set up to be successful in the long term and will lose the opportunity to learn about perseverance and grit. This player will also receive misleading feedback about how he or she is one of the best players. As flattering as this may appear to be, it might not have long-term benefits when other kids catch up to their size and speed. A youth sport coach needs to create an environment that is safe and productive for all participants, regardless of natural talent.

Losing games and experiencing athletes failing at basic skills is difficult for an untrained youth sport coach. There may a feeling that the lack of success reflects directly on them and their coaching, but they must come to see this as an opportunity to encourage players to embrace failure and use the failure as a learning opportunity for their future success. This is where the real learning occurs.

When this real learning occurs and the athletes are comfortable, athletes will become consistent winners in life as well as sports. Difficult to do as a coach when you feel like your team has to win so you can feel you beat the opposing team's coach and feel better about the handshake at the end of the game.

Winning as a coach means paving the way for the players to be focused on the process. That is when you gain real respect and admiration from the players. This is where you will have a platform to instill lifetime skills, such as being persistent, especially when failing, giving a great effort, staying positive, believing in yourself, and always directing your attention toward what is important. Something a youth sport coach did not sign up for, but comes with the responsibility of being called "coach," is the understanding that you are teaching values and habits that extend far beyond your games or contests.

How many times has a youth sport coach entered the single elimination playoff game, emphasized to the kids that this is really important, because if "we" lose our season is over? After this great speech, how many times has this emphasis resulted in a failure to execute the skills that were easy in the regular season?

This is a scenario that happens far too often in youth sports. Realizing that winning the championship is traditionally the goal can be a disaster for all involved. The coach at that point should give up focusing on the championship and instead focus on growing the roots of that championship team. Basically, anytime a coach focuses on and talks about winning, he or she has taken his team away from its highest level of play.

John Wooden defined the process orientation he used to structure his teams in his "Pyramid of Success." Coach Wooden defined success as "a piece of mind obtained only through self-satisfaction in knowing you made the effort to do the best of which you are capable." This is a brilliant way to suggest that a coach should emphasize the process.

Wooden uses this pyramid of success to teach his student athletes the value of a process approach to success. This set of values were important to him to pass on to each player. Coach Wooden shares this with us all in his book *Pyramid of Success*. This is a great read for all coaches who want to make their players into more successful people, well-rounded individuals, prepared for the next level of competition and, more than likely, winners.

GOAL SETTING

Goal setting has proven to be very effective. Any time an aim of an action is created, it gives a team direction. Being a professor of sport psychology, I can sense when the student athletes in my class are a bit more edgy as the weekend of their conference championship approaches. A win in the conference tournament equals an automatic birth into the national championship competition. This is a goal of every team on our campus.

While this goal can help motivate the soccer players to go on morning runs before the season in August, the goal of winning the conference championship can also have a negative effect on the morning of the conference championship match. If the athlete is focusing on this product goal during the competition, it takes precious energy away from that athlete being the best they can be in that moment. Any time an athlete is thinking about the past or the future during a competition, they are sacrificing valuable time to be their best in that moment. In this case, goal setting can result in greater anxiety.

These student athletes in my class speak of how important winning the conference championship and qualifying for the national championship is to their team. For sure, they do not want to be the ones to let their team down. However, after the team derived the goal of winning a conference championship they should have created the processes that will need to take place for that to happen and stay focused on those processes rather than the end goal.

What research has proven about these product or outcome goals at any age is that product goals can facilitate short-term motivation, but often lead to anxiety before and during competition. Goal setting is an extremely powerful technique for enabling athletes at any level to perform at their potential. However, it must be implemented correctly. Youth sport coaches who speak about winning or the importance of winning a specific competition are taking the participants away from their true potential.

Process goals, or performance goals, are more specific than product or outcome goals and are totally dependent on the actions of the participant. There is an ever-present opportunity for your youth sports teams to "win" all the time. Process goals of 100% dependent on the participant. Things have to happen outside of your players' control to achieve their product goals and to win all the time.

You certainly cannot control your opponent and they have a lot to do with whether or not you are going to win. Again, focusing on the product of winning has been proven to result in too much anxiety on the player. That is the point that the children are affected negatively and probably the reason most young participants abandon youth sports long before achieving their potential.

If the coach implements goals that are about the process, rather than the product, negative psychological factors, such as anxiety are lessened. The focus on process improves performance and most often results in the athlete feeling greater confidence and satisfaction. There is a continuous cycle going on between one's brain and body. Every thought that one has affects your body. Everything that goes in your mind affects your body. This is why we wake up in a sweat after having a bad dream. Also, everything that goes on in your body effects your thoughts. This mind-body cycle is very powerful and cannot be ignored by the youth coach.

When an athlete is uncomfortable and feels stress and anxiety over failing in a practice or contest, this negative mind-body cycle will affect their performance. If the structure you put in place as the coach assists your players in feeling safe and confident, they will experience positive thoughts. The brain will then send positive signals to the body and the body will reciprocate with positive signals back to the brain.

When the athlete feels good about their success, they will develop positive life skills that will be the foundation of their future success. This positive mind-body connection is what youth sports should be all about. At the point that this harmony between mind and body, thought and action is achieved, the coach will achieve the optimal learning environment for the athlete.

SUMMARY

- A coach should not focus on winning. A coach should emphasize a great structure and environment for the players to improve in and emphasize things the players can control such as believing in themselves, attitude and effort, communication, strategic decisions, fundamental movements, redefining the player's potential every day, and positive energy.
- A coach should keep consistent positive body language during competition. The coach should not react negatively to every bad play and questionable call by the official and like a fan when a team makes a good play.
- Even coaches that want to win in order to have the opportunity to coach at a higher level should not emphasize winning. By focusing on structuring your practices really well and emphasizing the process the coach will increase his or her chances of winning and gaining that promotion.
- If you find yourself competing against the other coach this is a clear indication that you need to focus on the process.
- When a coach creates a great structure for the team, emphasizes the process and his players feel comfortable and confident in, and the team experiences success, then the players will get excited and want to learn more. This is a great time for a coach to sell the process even more and gain some great momentum with the team.
- The Coach should define a win. Winning the controllables is a guaranteed win for the kids and good for their confidence and mental health
- If a coach is going to get angry or show frustration it should only be because one of the players or the coach did not focus on the process. Use errors as a learning opportunity.

- Goal setting can be effective to give initial direction and motivation but product goals, such as winning a championship, can be debilitating toward the team's success.
- Set goals that are process orientated.
- Goals that lead to stress and anxiety for your players during a competition should be avoided. The coach should not talk about these product goals and have goals in place to redirect the player's focus on the process or a performance.

Chapter 4

The Science about How Players Learn

What We Know about Motor Learning

MOTOR LEARNING RESEARCH

Research providing coaches with information on how players best learn to play the game is a must for new coaches at any level. Every move of an athlete is programmed in their mind and coaches at every level need to know the science behind that programming. Every time the athlete performs a skill a neurological movement pattern is reinforced in their mind. The more those specific nerves and impulses are used to make that movement pattern fire, the more automatic they become and the easier they become for the mind to repeat.

How is your breathing going? Breathing is a skill that you learn the instant you arrive in the world. The muscles that are required for breathing fire every time your brain dictates that you need to take a breath. You have performed this skill so well over such a long period of time it is automatic and part of your subconscious. You do not need to think about it.

Our goal as coaches, is to teach athletes movement patterns that use the best fundamentals of the skill, have them perform in the correct way so many times that it becomes as natural for them as breathing. The question is, what environment will best enable the coach to make that skill become automatic? The practice that a coach creates should include a structure and activities that enable the participants to learn the skill and automatically repeat the movement in a competitive environment.

Motor learning is a type of central representation (an image in the mind) that controls actions and movements. The actions and movements of an athlete (skill routines, fundamentals) are controlled by their motor programs. Obviously, the major job of a coach is making certain that athletes develop correct motor programs. When the athlete does not feel comfortable in the environment and fears failure, they will be unable to embed the proper motor patterns in their brains. That is why team culture is so important in coaching young athletes.

The absolute best environment for a youth sport participant to learn in does not include any sort of result or equipment that might give knowledge of result. A young basketball shooter would be better suited just learning the movements and not seeing whether or not the ball went in the hoop. Even if the ball was made for a beginner and the hoop was lower, when first learning the game, athletes would be better focusing on the motor patterns needed and not the results. The pure learning environment would include just the movement needed for the action. The anxiety of the result and the teacher's natural reaction to the result hinders performance.

Youth sport coaches do not have the opportunity to teach only movements first. Not only would parents and players think you were crazy, but the kids would be bored and not be prepared to compete with the preparation time allotted for most youth sports. However, realize that if you can teach the players the movements needed and the players are able to do them on their own at home, you will be setting the players up for long-term success. A good technique may be to start warm up at your practice with movements lasting only for five minutes.

When the athlete understands and feels safe in your practice, the coach has the opportunity to create a practice that will best help the athlete learn effectively. An educated youth sport coach knows the science behind learning and has researched the best fundamentals in their sport and can communicate these fundamentals quickly with great cues. Knowing these fundamentals clearly provides more time for the athletes to practice rather than listen to a lecture. Here is a list of motor development teaching parameters to remember when planning your practices.

IMAGE

First of all, please understand that the most impactful way youth sport participants learn is not from what you say but from what they see. My ten-year-old son will have a group of friends over playing basketball, and I am certain no youth sport basketball coach has ever taught a crossover dribble through your legs, step back three-point shot, but he and every one of his friends know how to perform this skill, and at a high level.

These young basketball players have watched their idol, Steph Curry, and after all of his YouTube videos, they have made his moves part of their neural patterns. The patterns that define Steph's sophisticated motor patterns are now in their automatic memories and they can do them without thinking.

They learned this move just by seeing Steph Curry perform it. If they had a mouthpiece hanging out of the side of their mouth you might not be able to tell them and Steph apart.

The image is the most powerful tool in learning. You would be better served as a youth sport coach to have a video screen of the best performer in whatever sport you are coaching at your practice rather than a sophisticated play book. After showing a video of the performer to the athlete, the natural question to start your practice would be, "Do you think you can do this movement exactly like the performer in the video?" Then the coach would be wise to add coaching tips based on the video.

This image and dialogue that you create to support it will increase the athlete's focus on the video. "See how the athlete is facing away from the bar before she jumps over it." (For high jump). Starting with a ten-minute lecture on how to execute the skill and sharing how brilliant you are at coaching is not the best way to teach young players the skills of their sport. It is difficult to hear, but great coaches are served well to understand how insignificant their explanations are and that can help them be more effective with visual images.

A great demonstration is helpful, and coaches might seek out an older sibling or an out-of-season varsity athlete to come and demonstrate the basic skill patterns of the sport to start a practice. If you know an elite performer (college athlete) who can come demonstrate to your young athletes the performance of the skill at a higher level, you may be able to make permanent a mental image that aids in helping athletes visualize optimum motor patterns.

TRANSFER

The best activities that a coach can do in a practice are the ones that reinforce the skills of the game and transfer to the team the skills needed for success in competitions. For example, I am confident to say that most of the basketball teams that have ever practiced in America have done the three-person weave. Yet, none of us have ever watched a basketball game and seen that movement repeated in a game situation.

Without being critical, I am not sure you have time to practice patterns that do not emerge in games. Basketball purists may argue that practicing the three-person weave is like reciting the creed in church, but there is no transfer from that drill to effective play during competition. You have to have activities in your practices that mimic the patterns your players are going to use in competition.

The basketball coach might defend the three-person weave drill in their practice plan by saying that it is an effective drill for passing, moving to the middle of the floor. If true, then the coach should practice those skills in the same setting the athletes are going to perform in during the competition. I have never seen three basketball players "weave" down the floor on a fast break.

Hitting off a tee in baseball or softball is similar. This skill is more like golf than baseball or softball. In a game, the batter is hitting a moving ball. Learning the skill of batting while hitting a moving or pitched ball is a far more effective way to teach hitting than hitting off a tee. With the amount of preparation time allotted for a season and the attention span of youth sport participants, a youth sport coach has little time to waste by practicing drills that have little or no transfer to competition.

WHOLE VS PART

If you want to learn how to play the piano, you do it by playing the piano. If you want to teach the players to play a sport, you have to learn by playing the sport that you are coaching. There is a methodology in coaching that focuses on learning parts of the skill and parts of the game, in a progression.

For example, if you wanted to teach a player how to pitch you would first start by having the player kneel and just flick their wrist. Then you would progress to a drill where the player moved their arm and continue to progress with many small drills that would eventually lead up to the player actually pitching the ball. As prevalent as this method is in America, this method of learning a skill may not be the most effective for the athletes.

Teaching parts of the skill or parts of the game does not prepare the players effectively for the skill that they need for the game. They are not learning the whole skill if they are not dealing with all the open ends of the skill when they are performing it. Many coaches break the skill down into these progressions, but research has proven this method of teaching is not the most effective way of teaching a skill. In reality, learning the skill in the whole game environment has proven to be the most effective way of teaching a skill.

Before youth sports boomed into the multibillion-dollar industry that it is today, two motor development researchers, Nixon and Licke, researched whole vs. part learning of skills. These researchers cited thirty whole-part studies, not one favored teaching methods that use the part method of instruction. Their research found that some variation of the whole method was associated with superior learning. This research helps cement the theory that youth sport participants need to practice the whole skill in the whole game setting rather than parts of the skill.

Coaches break down the skill into parts to teach parts of the skill before progressing to the whole skill. Teaching the part method can be effective to give athletes the feel for that movement pattern. However, coaches need to minimize the time that athlete practices the part methods compared to the whole skill. An elite team should devote 80% of their practice time to whole activities in practice, leaving 20% of their time for part activity. If the team is less skilled or beginners that percentage could change to 70% to 30%. Most importantly, the participants need to be learning and practicing skills needed for success in whole environments.

A specific example is that in volleyball many coaches start to teach players to spike by hitting the ball against the wall. This is good for the athlete to learn how to hit the ball, but the player should spend more time hitting the ball in the environment that they will need to in a game. They should practice hitting a ball that is set to them so they can learn to hit the ball when considering jumping, timing, and hitting over the net and other major considerations a spiker needs to learn.

Some sports are served well by teaching in progressions for safety consideration. Tackle football, for example, for safety reasons may use progressions. Most sports should put players in more game-simulated situations than progressions for ideal learning. Everything changes, when there is a defender in your face. Developing a practice environment that includes a whole environment should be part of your planning at every level.

STATE DEPENDENT REMEMBERING

When a player learns a skill, the state of the learning environment is remembered. This is a similar concept to whole vs. part learning. When an athlete is in a competitive environment, having practiced the movement pattern in that environment, results in better performance in game situations. It is challenging to create a game-like situation in practice but if you plan your practice correctly you can come close.

Quite simply, when a person learns something and it becomes part of their automatic memory, information about the environment in which the performance must occur matches the environment in which learning occurred. Performance is significantly better when the environment in which performance must occur matches the environment in which the learning occurred.

This is more evidence that progressions are not effective. The performer learns the skill better when preformed with all the unpredictable elements of the environment of which they are going to perform the skill. Youth sport athletes are better served when the coach matches the mood and feelings the athlete is going to experience in the competition to their practice situations.

MASS OR DISTRIBUTED PRACTICE

Research has proven that athletes, especially youth sport athletes, with a shorter attention span, benefit more from practicing a skill in increments of short time instead of the same amount of time spent in one block. For example, a tennis player could go to practice for ninety minutes with the goal of working on their serve, volleys, and backhand. Coaches might divide the practice into blocks of thirty minutes equally for each skill. These blocks might make beginning coaches feeling that they have touched on what their players need to be successful.

In reality, instead of having three blocks of thirty minutes for each skill, the athlete's learning curve would increase if the coach broke that time block up into three ten-minutes blocks repeated three times. Practicing each skill for ten minutes, in three practice blocks would be much more effective at making the skill automatic for the learner.

To start out with ten minutes of serving, followed by ten minutes of volleys, and lastly ten minutes of practicing backhand would increase the player's focus, attention to the cues, and generate enthusiastic positive energy toward the whole practice. Repeat this block three times. There is a point of diminishing returns on how long the athlete spends practicing each skill.

Distributing the execution and practice of the skill over time actually increases the athlete's focus and energy toward the skill. Just as we know that taking a five-minute walk every hour increases an adult's productivity at work, as presented in Daniel Pink's book, *When: The Scientific Secrets of Perfect Timing,* the same theory is just as true for athletes. For younger athletes, it is developmentally inappropriate for them to be expected to focus for these longer blocks of time that define too many youth practice plans.

Motor development research defines what are the appropriate movement patterns that can be expected at various ages. Developmentally appropriate coaching is a way of coaching that meets the participants where they are and demands that coaches need to know what can be expected of their participants physically and mentally at the level that they are coaching at.

A child that finishes the day at elementary or middle school needs a structure in youth sports that enables them to keep their focus after that day. At the end of a day, a structure that is set up poorly in a youth sport practice will cause the players to lose focus, and may result in that player eventually abandoning the sport they love.

For a youth sport participant, a coach should actually be crafting a practice of five- to ten-minute increments. Station work is the most effective tool for these practices. Even station work for three minutes that is focused on "part activity" gives players the opportunity for their brain to focus on the cues presented and then the transition to the next station providing a quick break for the brain. As long as the coach at the next station does not talk for more than ten seconds, (instructions or each station would be explained before the station activities), the players can get right into action and focus on the skill and its cues.

This quick-moving skills focus would be a good model for warm up and skill development so when athletes were placed in the "whole activity" during the practice, they will revert back to their station warm-up work and remember the moves they made with the proper cues. This is a far cry from working on one skill at the youth sport level for thirty minutes or even more than ten minutes.

OPPORTUNITIES TO RESPOND—"OTR"S

A good length of practice should not depend on the amount of time allotted; it should depend on how many repetitions the athlete received. Motor development scientists measure how many repetitions the athlete received in "opportunities to respond." When a practice is planned with these motor development strategies and the athletes have a lot of opportunities to respond, the coach can manage instruction time and transitions effectively. The end result is that athletes have a large percentage of activity time and little down time.

Activity time is the actual time the players are playing as opposed to listening, transitioning, or any activity that is not part of the sport. This is very important in a youth practice. Coaches can measure the activity time in their own practices. Just take the stopwatch or your phone and start the time when the athletes begin an activity and when they stop. You will most likely be shocked at what you find.

It is encouraged that you try this over several practices. Again, in a typical two-hour practice you will be surprised at how much time the participants are actually playing. An ideal amount of activity time is 80–90% activity in a practice. Most youth sport coaches who are starting out might find a practice is made up of only 30–40% of activity time. Some players might get more activity time than others and coaches should strive for all players getting 80–90% activity time.

If the coach is throwing batting practice to players in the cage and one player is batting at a time with five players waiting, the wait time those youth sport participants are experiencing is problematic. Too much wait time, with no structure in youth sport, will lead to off-task behavior and a lack of focus. This type of organization will most likely lead to a coach who just worked a full day to be frustrated. The players just went through that at school all day and need an active environment at youth sports that is structured to set them up for success.

A seven-year-old swim lesson, revealed in the example that follows, is one that should be avoided. Six swimmers are sitting on the edge of the pool and one teacher is in the water. The teacher gives instruction on how to kick the legs, then the teacher takes one swimmer at a time and works the leg kick with that swimmer for approximately 90 seconds. Then the teacher replaces the swimmer to their seat on the side of the pool and welcomes the next swimmer in the water to try the same thing for about the same time.

After giving all the kids time to work on the leg kick, the teacher would introduce the next skill then repeat the same process again. This sixty-minute swim lesson produces about ten minutes of activity time. Most of the time, the kids sit on the side of the pool, shaking with blue lips, because they are so cold. This example is not hypothetical, but one that I have lived through. Do not make it one that your athletes or their parents have to experience.

Coaches can modify the game so the youth sport athletes can get more activity time. Instead of a full field and full game of 11 vs. 11 soccer, the coach can play smaller games of 3 vs. 3 to get the players more touches on the ball. Coaches should not use activities that are just "part" of the entire skill that involve one ball and large lines. This wait time will cause everyone involved to be off task and away from their potential. Check your practice plan to make sure you have avoided these scenarios.

PRACTICE LENGTH

Why are 99% of practices at the youth sport level two hours long? Why are 99% of the practices at the high school level the same length of time? Why a large majority of coaches think that two hours is the magical time that you need to run a good practice? How can two hours be a great amount of time for a practice at the 6-year-old level and the college level? Typically, two hours is the length of time used for practices at all levels.

Youth sport coaches do not need 120 minutes to impart what players need to play a game. Parents are exhausted after work and taking care of their family. We know the energy it takes to plan and manage a youth sport practice is demanding but think in your planning how challenging the practice you create is for parents as well as your athletes. Dinner is an important meal for everyone.

When you plan, put yourself in the shoes of a nine-year-old. After a day of being cramped up in a classroom going through the productivity line of education, all the while looking out the window, dying to be outside, the young athlete finally gets to your practice. Your practice should be exciting and be the highlight of the day. However, going to a practice that is not a safe environment, that has no definitive culture that emphasizes the process and learning, that has low activity time and poor management, that last much longer than the time that young person can developmentally endure, will destroy the love of the sport.

If you run your practices effectively, you can get more effective activity in ninety minutes than in two hours. If you managed the team well and transitioned effectively, meaning all the equipment was ready and in place, the coaches were prepared, players' groups organized, you could actually run a great youth sport practice in sixty minutes. Your practice should be so much fun, that you leave the athletes dying to come back for more! Two hours being the ideal time is a myth with no science behind it. If you organize your practice well and get your practice time down to sixty minutes, you will be more successful in the end. Less is more.

MOTOR DEVELOPMENT CONCEPTS

All the concepts touched on in this chapter are factors to consider when you make your practice plan. Coaches should always have a plan for practice that includes the activities but also includes transitions (moving players from one activity to another), groups, objectives, and all the coach's roles. The thing about coaching is that it is hard to regroup a team after organization has failed.

Coaching is like oil painting. You have this blank canvas (the first day of practice) and every stroke you paint will be a part of the final painting. Every decision you make, every minute of every practice, will affect your team. There is no white out. You need to stay on top of your organization from the beginning. Once the culture is set and the coach shares the structure they are going to use for the team, you are on your way to a successful experience for you as well as your young athletes.

If you are aware of the situation (statistic) that most directly correlates to the success of your team, you should work on that part of the game the most. A block plan is when a coach creates activities that the team needs to work on and this should be centered on what they need for success. You can evaluate the last practice or competition and decide what your team needs to get better at in planning the coming practice. A block plan can cover a single practice or you can plan all the activities you think you are going to need to practice over a longer period of time.

Here is a sample block plan for a 10–12-year-old little league baseball team. This team has nine practices before its first competition.

Items to work on in rank order of importance—Spend the most time in practice on most important items in rank order:

1. Pitching
2. Catching
3. Hitting
4. Infield—Ground Balls
5. Outfield—High Pops
6. Cut offs
7. Throwing motions—This can be covered in warm up short time and reinforced during practice
8. Base running—how to attack
9. Base running situations how to defend

Practice 1
Pitching
Catching
Hitting
Infield
Outfield
Cut offs
Throwing Motion

Practice 2
Pitching
Catching
Hitting
Base running attack
Base running defend

Practice 3
Pitching
Catching
Hitting
3 teams rotating—script situations

Practice 4
Pitching
Catching
Hitting
Infield
Outfield

Cut offs

Practice 5
Pitching
Catching
Hitting
Base running—defend
Base Running—attack
2 strike hitting

Practice 6
Pitching
Catching
Hitting
Situation game play

Practice 7
Pitching
Catching
Hitting
Game Play

Practice 8
Pitching
Catching
Hitting
Scrimmage

Practice 9
Scrimmage

From that block plan the coach can design practice plans for each day. The block plan might change. In this case with baseball, maybe you will lose a practice day due to rain. You do not need to make a practice plan for each day because you can lose a practice or you might want to change the block plan but the practice plan needs to be made before the practice and shared with the coaches before the practice.

When you make a practice plan for each day incorporating all the skills you need to work on in that practice, you can review all the motor development concepts and see if they were applied to the practice plan. This practice plan covers the objectives of the block plan. The practice plan would be shared with the coaches before practice. The coaches would bring a copy of the practice plan to practice and then the coaches would meet for 5 minutes before practice to make sure everyone understood their roles and how all the transitions will work in order to have a great practice for the kids.

Here is what a good practice plan would look like. It is made from the "Practice 1" of the block plan. You can see all the objectives in "Practice 1" are covered in this practice plan with correct motor learning principles with a good structure for the players.

DATE: THR June 7 *TIME*: 6–7:30
EQUIPMENT: 2 Buckets of Balls—1 extra bucket—Core Coach Charlie, Mike, Ed, Todd
Value sheets
Have code for equipment box at the field
Coach Objectives: Organized, fast tempo practice, a lot of reps
Feedback—Be specific positive—Not "Good hit," change to "Way to keep your hands high" "Nice 1 move to the ball"—If you have a corrective statement use a positive 1st—"Great hands high—Keep your hands above the ball." Fast
2 Strike Strategy = expand the strike zone and get the ball in play

6:00–6:01—Review Core Values—Fast tempo, Deliberate challenge—MOVING FAST
Player groups GROUP 1 (Seamus—JD—Connor L—Jackson) GROUP 2 (Justin L—Carter—Quinn—Will) GROUP 3 (Simon R—Kyle—Patrick—Gavin)

6:01–6:10—Warm up in 3 groups—2 of 4 and 1 of 5
Base running from home to 2nd—Aggressive round 1st base—50%, 75%, 100% intensity gradually increase—Coach Todd
Pop Ups—Coach on Right field Line—Player 10 feet away—Turn and jog to right—coach leads him with a pop up. Catch run back to coach—Coach gets next player going before player who caught the ball gets the ball back to him—Careful not to throw arms not loose—Coach Mike
Shuffle grounders—short and third base—Ready position—shuffle behind the ball left and right—set your feet and 2/3 steps toward first base—stepping toward first—Coach Charlie & Ed
3 minutes each station and rotate—Coaches explain station when players arrive—Charlie time

6:10–6:20—Throwing warm up—Left field foul line—Have balls there and ready—Cues "Get Set Up" "Let me see your arm pit"
10 feet—3 minutes—Change partners each day

Box throwing Drill (Throw in a box)—in your groups—change direction—3 mins

"11"—come from ground ball position throw to your partner—hit chest = 2 pts, face = 1, anything else = 0 points—first one to 11 wins—in partners—4 mins

6:20–6:50—3 At soft toss net—Demo batting cues 1. Loaded 2. Hands at ear "Listen to the shell" 3. On top of ball—Hands barometer—above = ball, keep hands above the ball—one simple move down to the ball—Good for 1st day.

Station 1—Soft toss with Coach Ed—45-degree angle—hand extended—have kids see pitcher 1st and then pick up ball—move their head. Each player gets 2 inside, 2 outside, 2 high, 2 low—all with batting cues = remind players—Really want to see more batters making one, quiet move to the ball with their hands

Station 2—Four-way fungo infield practice—Mike and Todd

Station 3—Pop up cues—1. Still on hitter contact 2. Feet to ball 3. Glove to ball 4. 2 hands 5. Crow hop toss—Coach Charlie

SAME GROUPS

6:50–7:30—Game hitting and fielding

Play "THUNDER"—Charlie explains

Coach Todd pitches

Fielders have to achieve an objective—batter hits and runs to get as many bases as possible before fielding team completes the objective—total the number of bases the runners get for team score

1 group of 4 up—batters' bat with 2 strikes—rotate groups that bat

Team's deliberate goal for entire scrimmage—field 70% ground balls cleanly—Ed stat on clipboard

Fielders 1st Objective

Ball has to throw to right fielder—right fielder hit cut off player 2nd base—to third base—third base apply tag—Batter runs past home and get 5 bases at first

Fielders 2nd Objective

Ball to left field and cut off for home catcher applies tag—Coach Ed

Fielders 3rd Objective

Ball has to go to center—cut third and third basemen then has to turn a double play

Team at bats for 6 minutes

Get as many at bats as you can

Each team bats twice

Biggest cue—hands one quiet move to the ball
Teams keep their total score
Coaches coaching:
> Todd pitching—hitting cuts
> Charlie—infielders lining up cuts
> Ed—outfielders—still on contact and hitting cuts

Charlie and Ed can relieve Todd if necessary

AT SAME TIME——7 players in the field—Coach Mike takes one player at a time to work on pitching—Mike grabs players—Mike can catch and review cues—Mike come up with 3 cues that you would work on with these pitchers.

7:30—Parents pick up players

SUMMARY

- Use the science of learning movements when creating drills and activities for practice.
- Create an environment that athletes feel comfortable learning movements and learning from mistakes.
- The image is the most powerful learning tool for the learner. Demonstrations and videos are useful.
- The drills the team does in practice should reflect the movements and environment the athletes are going to see in the game so their learning transfer well into competition.
- Practice the whole game in practice with objectives to focus on certain skills and modifications to increase repetitions.
- Drills should have same game settings as competitions.
- To work on a skill in shorter time periods repeated increases learning rather than one long-time block.
- Youth sport participants need a structure that will help them maintain focus and not allow them to get off task very easily.
- To increase "opportunities to respond" (OTRs) coaches should increase equipment, use smaller lines, have multiple activities, and play smaller sided games in practice.
- 2-hour practices are too long for youth sport participants.

Chapter 5

Competition and Deliberate Goals

How to Increase Focus in Your Practice

COMPETITION

In the original Latin origin for the word, *competition*, you will find the words striving and together. These words are important for coaches to understand in dealing with and teaching about competition with their teams. If two players are competing for playing time at the same position, when one gets better, the other will have to improve in order to stay competitive.

If the second player improves and is playing better than the first player, the first player would have to further improve to stay competitive. In this case these two players are pushing each other to higher levels of performance and if this is happening around the whole team, then the players and the whole team are "striving together."

In the same way, young players should be taught that their opponents are not the enemy, but that a good opponent will force them to improve as a team. Rather than seeing the opposing team has something to destroy, teams should be taught that they are actually "striving together" with the other team in the pursuit of excellence. Just as a competitive teammate demands that they perform a higher level, they should come to see the opposing team as offering them an opportunity to bring out the best in both them and their team.

Another key to competitive situations on teams is whether the coach creates an environment that encourages competition while also developing team cohesion and cooperation. Can the coach inspire players to both compete with each other and encourage one another? When competition is seen as a threat or causes strife between players, then it hurts the overall team's performance. A coach is responsible for encouraging competition along with cooperation and cohesion within the team.

The sample practice plan in the last chapter included competition in the activities. There was a point total accumulation system in the throwing warm up, and in "Thunder," the last activity. In those situations, there were three teams competing to see how many points they could score at bat and performing to achieve the specific objectives in the field to keep their opposition from scoring when batting. Introducing competition in your practice helps the players focus and develop their skills. Practicing in a competitive environment also transfers well into the games. How well your activities transfer is always an important consideration in practice planning.

It is one thing to develop coordinated fundamental moves for the athletes on your teams, but there is another type of coordination called "competitive coordination." Some form of competition, where there is someone else, who can measure and evaluate performance, even coaches, makes the environment that the skill is being performed in more competitive. Competitive coordination adds a whole other layer to performing.

For example, I can praise the basketball player for making a free throw but if that athlete does not practice that free throw in a competitive environment, when there is one second left in a game, your team is down two and that athlete is on the line, she or he will not be prepared. If the practice environment has no competition and consequence, there will be no transfer or the "state dependency" of the training would not match the competition. In the competition, the athlete needs "competitive coordination" to perform the movement successfully.

Therefore, the coach needs to create competition in practice for the athletes to practice in that simulates the game situations that they will face. It will be difficult to perfectly match the competitive environment that teams face, but any form of competition goes a long way, even if the uniforms are not on. It does not have to be something of enormous consequence, but a little consequence, like five push-ups for the losers or the winner does not have to pick up the balls, gives the athlete the reality of the event.

This suggestion may seem to be in contrast to the earlier chapter on how to define winning, but it really is not. Coaches should not emphasize winning games but should always have players focus on the process. Winning and losing the game are ultimately part of this focus on practicing a process. We are not trying to crown a winner by having a competition, rather we just want the environment in which the player is learning and performing that matches the one that they will compete in during competitions with other teams.

Competition prepares the youth sport participants for life. When the participants learn to compete in a safe environment, they practice life lessons of grit, perseverance with failure, and hard work. Competition is fun and youth sport participants list competition as a major reason for participating. There are amazing lifelong lessons that come from competition when the youth sport leader provides the opportunity to compete in an emotionally sound environment.

In addition, competition gives the performer authentic practice that simulates actual contests. Even though there is a scoreboard, we want to emphasize, not on the end result of a game, but instead invest in all the things the athlete can control such as staying confident, believing in oneself, having good positive energy, not thinking about and relying on the training they have had, but unlocking their subconscious performance.

By structuring a practice with competition, the coach gives the athlete the opportunity to train with focus. Focus is staying positive and connected to the objective in the face of obstacles that might distract attention, which is exactly what the athlete will need to do to make both two free throws in a pressure packed situation.

DELIBERATE GOALS

Introducing deliberate goals is another way a coach can help an athlete maintain his or her focus in practice. When we define focus as staying positive and connected to the objective, we are teaching a unique and vital aspect of focus. In general, very few athletes perform better when they are angry or frustrated. Therefore, the angrier they get, the more their performance deteriorates. Having a core value that states the importance of focusing on the process and not choosing anger is important so your players will have the best chance to perform to their potential. In reality, anger is one letter away from *Danger* for your players.

A youth sport participant that has a competitive spirit is a great asset for a team. The athlete that competes with excitement or anticipation of doing his or her best is on track for a successful career. Choosing anger is usually the result of an exaggerated concern about the end product or the result of the game, the score. Losing track of the process causes the athletes to choose behaviors not aligned with the team's core values and generally destructive of team play.

The coach should refer the athletes back to the team's core values of when experienced athletes getting off track. The youth sport participant with a positive competitive spirit should be given positive reinforcement for competing with a good process that mirrors core values. This player and play should even be highlighted as a positive leader and an example for other players.

Excitement can facilitate confidence, performance, and pleasure. This is all part of the structure that the coaches set up from the first practice. If the coach has a structure that allows players to feel safe, even when they lose in practice, they should still feel excited and even learn to complement, support, and encourage the winner. This positive approach allows the athletes to be cognitive of the objective. Anger is an emotion that takes away our intellectual capabilities and makes staying connected to an objective difficult, usually leading to more anger and danger.

There is a good way to balance sportsmanship and competition together in a practice game situation. In a scrimmage or game at a youth level, when one team has significantly more talent than the other and is crushing them on the scoreboard, stop the scrimmage and bring in the players. Ask for a volunteer from the dominant team to move to the weaker team to balance the team strength of both teams.

When you first institute this practice, almost no one will want to make the switch, but multiple experiences using this method has shown that the best competitors will eventually see it as a badge of honor to move to the less talented team and even will strive to move the balance of power and win the game. When that competitive player switches teams he or she is on a mission to compete by influencing others to chose the process. Having the players lead each other successfully through the process is powerful.

After a few times doing this in practice, or even in games with weaker opponents, every athlete will enthusiastically volunteer to be a sportsmanship ambassador and switch teams. At this point as youth coach, you have succeeded in having your players learn the true meaning of competition, striving together, to get better. By the way, this may be the most valuable thing you can do to develop your better players as they now have to strive against stronger players and teams, which they will most certainly face as they move on in the sport.

Deliberate goals help the players and the team focus on a specific skill. By introducing a deliberate goal, the coach triggers the direction and intensity of the team's focus. Instead of mindless repetitions, the deliberate goal gives the activity great purpose creating a more competitive situation. For example, instead of practicing passing in lacrosse, the coach can say that partners should make fifteen successful passes in a row, while moving from twenty feet to forty feet. This deliberate goal instantly gives the activity more purpose and has the practice environment set up and feel more like a competition.

Over a period of time that a team is engaged in a "whole activity" that is modified to increase repetitions and "opportunities to respond," a coach can set deliberate goals. For example, in the baseball scrimmage activity, "Thunder," at the end of the sample baseball practice plan shown in the last chapter, the coach has a deliberate goal of fielding ground balls successfully 70% of the time.

This is a team deliberate goal where the coach can update the team during the thirty-minute activity. In lacrosse, one coach can track ground balls taken and track how many were successfully taken on the first touch. As the scrimmage progresses, the coach can yell out the score after every ground ball, "5 out of 7." By yelling out the score the player's focus is redirected toward the deliberate goal at which point they should remember the cues in hopes of making a successful movement pattern, increasing focus.

"Team, we are at 65% and we have 10 minutes left, lets move our feet on those ground balls and get to our deliberate goal of 70%." At the end of the activity, if the team accomplishes the goal, there can be a celebration and if they did not meet their goal, there can be a minor consequence, five push-ups or a minor exercise.

You can see how this deliberate goal helps give the group overall direction, intensity, and purpose. We can practice with mindless repetitions in practice and hope that the skill goes well in the competition or we can find out specifically how well the skill is going in practice setting the goal of achieving a deliberate goal related to that project.

When creating deliberate goals, you should look at identifying the skills most crucial to your team's success, statistically what level to perform that skill at that correlates to winning. You have to do some research in your sport. Sometimes, this is as simple as asking some people who have coached a team in the league before or seeking out the director of the league to discover the key skill that you need to work on for success in your sport. Overall, having a deliberate goal really helps the participants to enjoy your practices and give them more direction.

Choosing the goal is one of the keys to implementing this skill, but highlighting the athletes who need work is another consequence of deliberate goals. Deliberate goals can vary from individual to partner to team goals. Be aware of the youth sport participant who is not as skilled as the other, whose errors are making it difficult for the team to achieve these goals. If your core values include encouragement this would be a good time for the teammates to reach out to this player. Also, have one of the coaches give this player encouragement and extra individual attention.

The percentage surrounding the goal that you choose could also be below a standard that you think is necessary, but fair in reflecting all the players and how they perform on your team. This situation is a good reason for not have a running total for the "whole" activity. Relaying to the team periodically reinforces the group's focus and does not highlight errors by any one player, making them uncomfortable.

Below is another sample practice plan with examples of deliberate goals. You can also go back and review motor development concepts covered in chapter 4. The organization of the players in certain groups are done in the planning stage and not during practice, wasting valuable time. This avoids confusion and a lack of activity time for the players. A good rule of thumb is to have practice include a lot of repetitions and not a lot of conversations. Conversations are for after practice. Diagrams can help to diminish confusion on how the activities will go. This practice plan was created with "Practice 2" objectives from the block plan in chapter 4.

DATE: Friday June 9   *TIME*: 6–7:30
EQUIPMENT: White Board—Core Value sheets—"You De Man" Expectations—TENNIS BALLS
Coaches—Todd—Mike—Ed—Todd bring Hula Hoops
"You De Man" award given at the end of practice to the player best exemplifying hustle, positive attitude, helping others, and all core values. Coaches will choose together. Tell the players this is going to happen before practice starts.

6:00–6:01—Review Core Values—Review You De Man—MOVING FAST
Player groups
  GROUP 1 Justin L—Will P—Carter—Patrick
  GROUP 2 Javier—Lawrence—Simon—Jose
  GROUP 3 Sheamus—JD—Quinn—Monte

6:01–6:15—throwing warm up—Left field foul line—Have balls there and ready—Cues "Get Set Up" "Let me see your arm pit"
10 feet—3 minutes—new partner
Game to 11—3 minutes—(same as last practice competition)
   Box throwing—players form a box and throw around the square
Line Relay—3 things you are saying "Hit Me"—"Left/Right"—"Cut 2/3/4"—Nothing throw through

6:15–6:30—Bunting and base-running strategy and defense.
8 fielders 4 bunters—Bunt defense and bunt practice and base running situations—players bunt into the hula hoops placed on the ground.
Coach Todd and Coach Mike explain—3 cues and get practice—Keep rotating bunters through
Coach Todd pitch—Coach Mike Coach bunters
Coach Ed Coach runners—Coach Charlie explain defense cues—Deliberate Goal 70%—clean throws to first, Coach Charlie stat
Station 1—Soft toss with Coach Ed—45 degree angle—hand extended—have kids see pitcher 1st and then pick up ball—move their head. Each player gets 2 inside, 2 outside, 2 high, 2 low—all with Batting cues = remind players—Really want to see more batters making one, quiet move to the ball with their hands

Station 2—Infield practice with Coach Charlie and Coach Mike—Cues for ground balls and throwing

Station 3—Coach Todd pitching tennis balls—Hit a laser stay another pitch—Not a laser then change batter—Non batters line up on the fence. Batter on foul line—Coach Mike pitch while taking a knee. Group shags tennis balls when done—From right field line—Short distance fast darts

SAME GROUPS

6:35—6:55—3 groups rotate—6 minute stations
Station 1—Coach Ed into cage in left field—have bucket of balls ready
Station 2—Home plate and infield with Coach Charlie and Coach Mike—6 balls ready
Station 3—Tennis balls in bag—Coach Todd on right field line—have players run to shag in 15 seconds

6:55–7:30
"13"—Need 13 points before 3 outs
Points—Single = 1, Double = 2, Triple = 3, Homer = 4, Lazor hits or opposite field shot outside pitch = 4. Coach can award randomly based on their judgment.
Coach pitch and judge
Players stay in groups (steady catches) and once a team gets 13 or 3 outs then have them transition in 15 seconds. Count it out.
Coach Todd pitch—Coach Charlie infield—Coach Ed cut offs—Coach Mike work with catcher
Deliberate Goal—hit cut off player 90% of the time.
Closure: Coaches discuss who to give "You De Man" award to and share with team. Review cues and core values. Share "You De Man" was a tough decision because a lot of great performances.

7:30—Parents pick up—90 minute practice.

SUMMARY

- Competition is defined as "striving together." The teammates and opponents players compete with give them a great opportunity for improvement and growth.

- Coaches need to create activities and whole games in practice that transfer well into competition.
- When introducing competition coaches should remind players to focus on the process and the things they can control and not the scoreboard.
- Use deliberate goals in practice to increase player's focus on achieving a part of the game that correlates strongly to success in competition.
- Coaches should make practice plans and organize players and coaches' roles before practice and share with coaches before practice. Practice plans should also include equipment necessary, transitions, objectives from a block plan, motor learning principles, whole activities instead of part activities, how the team will compete in a game setting and deliberate goals.

Chapter 6

Communication and Feedback

The Art and Science of How You Should Talk to Players

COMMUNICATION

Communication is key in any relationship and a great coach will always be labeled as a great communicator. Coach, is really a term of endearment. For you to accept the responsibility of being called, Coach, you must be willing to honor the player-coach relationship. Improving your communication skills are your first priority.

Your communication starts by sharing the core values of your team as you communicate what behaviors are expected and are important. In accepting the title of Coach, you must be prepared to put a lot of time into communicating with your players. The more time you put into effectively communicating with your players, the stronger your relationships will grow.

The way to get the trust of all your players is to communicate effectively. From the start of the season, it is imperative to share your expected behaviors through your core values, introducing skills and cues as well, refining performance and behavior and evaluating future areas of improvement with the team.

When you are sharing the structure that you are setting up, the players (even the players with less skill) will start to experience success in your environment and at that point you can really start to generate momentum toward a unique and special team. Your players will start to believe in everything that is going on and will become enthusiastic about participating. This enthusiasm is a result of the participants feeling excited about the team structure you created as a coach. It is fun to play on a good team.

One challenge a youth sport coach has is that not all the participants have the same enthusiasm toward playing. For the player, who may not be as motivated, the coach will need a great structure and should be prepared to communicate a good deal more with these players. Communication is the key to your players buying in more. As the team generates enthusiastic momentum, all the players, regardless of ability, will become more excited. It takes work but that is a responsibility you took on as coach when you volunteered to run the team.

A system that has little structure, with activities that are not appropriate for the age level, with teaching cues that are not creative or effective, will result in players becoming less engaged. A superior structure with great communication, helps all the players, and creates a situation that players will be enthusiastic about. These practices can eliminate the typical coach frustration in dealing with the players who display an attitude that they do not want to be involved. The coach is responsible for the team environment and everything that a coach does contributes positively or negatively toward all the player's enthusiasm.

Once you have established a strong team bond, an added bonus will result. Your opponents will recognize that they do not have the same positive structure and it can shake their confidence. Your positive structure can start to generate compound team cohesion, and your team will start to take off. We all know nothing great ever happened without enthusiasm from Ralph Waldo Emerson. Be prepared to come to practice and have small conversations with each player multiple times as they arrive. You should see yourself as a salesperson for enthusiasm, always selling your love of the game and coaching to the players.

As much as the coach has to communicate extensively with the players, the coach also has to communicate well with all the other coaches. Coaches all have different roles. Some might be primary teachers and others might just be helping to facilitate the activities. If the coaches are going to be coaching the players, then the head coach must always be putting attention toward educating and managing the staff.

The head coach can use emails during the day to share practice plans and agenda items with the team and staff. In today's world, with older players, group texts have replaced email. The coaches should huddle quickly before practice to make sure the plan is clear and everyone understands the objectives and what their role in the practice will be. Also, after practice, it is important to evaluate what went well and what changes are necessary. Individual conversations between the head coach and other coaches are necessary to keep everyone working together as a cohesive staff.

If coaches are co-coaching, the head coach must ensure that everyone's responsibilities are clear. If one coach is responsible for bringing the equipment, the head coach must ensure that that coach is responsible and does not forget. If another coach is responsible for sharing the practice plan, then the head coach must ensure that he does his job. Together, the coaches can decide what the "block plan" is going to be and what needs to be worked on next, but the head coach should create the final plan for practice. Many youth sport coaches do not arrive at practice with a practice plan written out. That is a disaster waiting to happen.

FEEDBACK

The skill of giving feedback to players is something that all coaches need to work on and perfect, if they are to become successful. Inexperienced coaches most often demonstrate their lack of experience in how they talk to players. A coach has to say the right thing, and they have to say it correctly, relaying their message in a way that is not too long or too short, not too fast or too slow. This is not easy. It is both a science and an art. If we know that the image is the most powerful learning tool, we also know that the only weapon the coach has to change performance and behavior is their voice and the words they choose to use. Feedback is the key to great coaching.

Coaches should be aware of how much they are talking during the entire practice. An instruction or introduction of an activity has to be complete with clear objectives, but not too long. This is not a lecture; this is practice. A coach needs to realize the nuances that are worth repeating and those that should be avoided. Some coaches say "ok" multiple times a practice or some repeat, "c'mon," 500 times in every practice. These patterns are difficult for players to listen to every practice. It is a good practice to think about how much your players like hearing from you and what your speech is like during a practice.

If you ever wonder what you voice sounds like, just hold your cell phone in your hand and record the practice. You can gain a lot of information from listening to the recording. In some cases, you are not going to believe what you sound like. Also, you can tally anything that you want to further develop in your coaching as well as those things in your speech to eliminate.

ROSENTHAL EFFECT

Robert Rosenthal the originator of the Pygmalion effect performed a research study that has such consistent and profound results that the results have simply become known as the Rosenthal effect. Originally, the experiment was done with lab rats. Students were in charge of caring and training lab rats who were being trained to run through a maze. The students had to clean their cages and train them in the maze. Rosenthal kept the rats in two separate groups.

Rosenthal introduced group A to the trainers as "maze bright" and group B as "maze dull." The rats were chosen randomly. There was no such thing as some rats who were better or worse at completing the maze. Over a period of time, the rats that were in the "maze bright" group out performed the rats in the "maze dull" group consistently 100% of the time. The rats in group A went faster through the maze. Just by reading the sign on the cage and having a belief of what kind of rat they were dealing with, the students treated and had different expectations for each group. Therefore, the rats performed differently.

Rosenthal then performed a similar experiment in elementary schools and found the same results. Even though a group of students had been chosen randomly, because the teachers believed they were smarter and able to learn better, those students performed better on IQ tests at the end of the year. Rosenthal has performed this experiment in many fields and found consistent results. Our beliefs about a person's abilities effect our actions and how we treat those people.

This is important for coaches to realize. What if we believed the worst performer on our team had the most potential. Our behaviors toward that player would be different. Therefore, do not give up or consistently treat any player as if they have no hope. Your judgment will have an effect on them. Treat all your players as if they have the ability to be the best. Your actions will not only impact their season but the foundation for their belief in themselves for a lifetime.

SIMPLE/CONSISTENT

All coaches on a team need to speak the same language. It is imperative that for each skill taught, all the coaches know what the skill cues are that they are going to be teaching and the coaches only talk about those skill cues with the same language. This is why it is important that the skill cue phrases are clear before the season begins.

If a coach is coaching a player to accomplish one of the cues, then they need to only share feedback in the same language on that particular cue. If the session involves station work and each station has an objective then the coach should only review the specific objective particular to that station, even if the coach notices other cues not being done well, they must leave them for another practice.

Keep it simple. For an athlete to hear three things to work on at once is confusing and overwhelming. The athlete will make more improvement by focusing on one cue at a time. It is challenging for a coach not to talk about other cues as they see could be improved in a performance but keep focusing on one cue at a time to help the athlete.

Be patient. Often times, coaches get excited to share all their knowledge, they talk about too many things at once or go rogue and start to talk about cues that are not a part of the team's vernacular. Keep it simple, one cue will take care of a lot of problems and with your feedback will solve a lot of problems.

One way to ensure consistency is for the coaches to make time outside of practices to meet together to be sure that they are emphasizing the same things, with the same language. This preparation will help you keep your feedback simple and consistent. Quick Zoom calls make this meeting easy.

A team with no organization will have coaches think of things to talk about on the spot. That might work in rare occasions in the short term, but in the long term, having greater organization will help your players develop more rapidly. If you think that your team is not getting better at a skill as quickly as the coaching staff had hoped, you can add another cue, but it would be done in uniformity within the coaching staff. Even though there must be cooperation and joint planning within the staff, the final decisions must always be made by the head coach.

SKILL ANALYSIS

When you watch an athlete perform a skill, you are actually analyzing what is going well and what needs to be worked on. The only way to get efficient at skill analysis is to watch more so that you can facilitate improvement. When you are familiar with the cues that you are going to be teaching you know what to look for. When you measure a fundamental move by a performer you are determining what can be done better. If you are looking for one or two cues that give you direction, you are observing a performer to evaluate what you are going to provide feedback about.

There will be times when the performance is so bad you don't know where to start. What should you do in these cases? You can do one of two things. You can refine a cue that takes place in the early or in the first phase of the skill or you can choose to correct the biggest error. All skills have a series of phases that are usually preparation and ready position, force producing phase, execution, and follow through phase.

If you analyze that everything is going poorly then start with a cue that will most likely help the performance. Or you could choose the biggest error. By correcting the biggest error of the skill performance, you would be helping the performer get closer to learning the correct fundamental movement.

It is good to watch the athlete perform the skill three to five times before you decide what you are going to provide feedback about. After determining what feedback is going to help this performer reach a higher level, you are ready to give your feedback. Again, make it quick. We do not want to take repetitions away from the athlete. After you give your feedback, you should watch another couple of repetitions. Many times, a coach will give feedback and then start to observe another performer. It is best to watch the performer after you give feedback to be able to follow up, either praising the change, or continuing to work on the feedback about the movement.

KNOWLEDGE OF RESULTS (KR) OR KNOWLEDGE OF PERFORMANCE (KP)

When a coach gives feedback about the skill cues, they are helping the performer. This type of feedback is called knowledge of performance (KP) feedback. Knowledge of performance feedback deals with the process the athlete is going through. Even if the coach is giving positive feedback, they should talk about the process. Not only does the athlete you are talking to receive help, but the other players on the team hear the content of the feedback and the statement becomes a learning opportunity for them as well.

The opposite of KP feedback is knowledge of results (KR) feedback that deals with the result. "Nice hit," "Good catch," "Great serve," or "Awesome job" are all statements that deal with the result. When a foul shooter hits the front rim and the coach says, "A little farther," this result-centered feedback is shallow. It also repeats what the athlete already knows. The ball hit the rim. There is nothing in that statement that gives the performer more knowledge than they already have or encourages the player. They can see the effort did not generate enough power. They don't need a coach to share what they already know.

What the athlete needs is a coach to guide them through learning the process. A coach who gives information about the movement is helping the player build a repeatable pattern that will enable them to be successful over time. Therefore, it is a waste of time for a coach to repeat information that athlete already knows. Invest in your athlete's future more by providing accurate, insightful feedback about their movement. Repeat the skill cues that you have researched and use them as feedback. They are a shared language.

POSITIVE SPECIFIC FEEDBACK

Feedback has gone through a timeline over the years. The days of a coach talking and barking demands as a dictator would, as in the case of the legendary Bobby Knight, are past us. Bobby Knight was a very successful men's basketball coach at University of Indiana, who was very demanding and did not concern himself with the athlete's feelings, rather he just supplied the information needed to improve performance.

If what Coach Knight yelled was demeaning for the player, then too bad for the athlete. Making his athletes better was his main objective and his motive was to improve performance without worrying about the player's feelings. He was a yeller and what he said, the athlete did, or the athlete suffered. For some players, this system was effective and Knight's methods were emulated by coaches around the nation. For others, this type of feedback was destructive and actually detrimental to performance.

As time went on, coaches started to move away from this type of unfeeling feedback, realizing that no one likes to be controlled or humiliated, and that this approach was ineffective, and abusive on some levels. Everyone responds to positive feedback. Coaches began to talk differently to the athletes, in part, based on behavioral research.

Based on these trends, coaches started to supply a lot of positive feedback on every level of sport. In the NFL, some coaches started to be labeled as "player coaches." Steve Mariucci of the San Francisco 49ers was one of the first of these coaches and his success led to coaches beginning to direct feedback in more positive, educational terms rather than the discipline-driven feedback that might have been the norm in the Bob Knight era. Bill Walsh references positive feedback in his book *Winning Philosophy of Bill Walsh*.

These coaches reflect kind, intelligent, collegial teachers rather than antagonistic taskmasters, who control players and their movements. The positive feedback movement took coaching in a positive direction, but we have to realize that generic positive feedback is not always valuable to an athlete. Just being positive is not always the most effective feedback that the player needs to hear.

Positive specific feedback is what a coach needs to strive for. What positive specific feedback means is the that coach utilizes being positive to enhance the environment for the players, but the feedback provided is specific. The feedback concerns what the athlete did well and again this optimizes learning opportunities for everyone on the team.

A coach who gives positive specific feedback helps motivate the players and the coach who gives positive feedback about exactly what the athlete did well is supplying KP information that helps the athlete, and the team, get excited about making and repeating the proper movement. Again, the other players who hear this feedback benefit from an indirect learning experience as well.

Some coaches believe that positive feedback is always helpful, but that is not true. A soccer coach who offers the feedback, "Great shot," is providing what is called blanket positive feedback. From that feedback, players may come to believe that they are a great shooter or goal scorer. Inexperienced coaches use blanket positive feedback excessively, often thinking the athletes are benefiting from their generic positive feedback. The athletes most likely will react happily to this feedback, but in the long term, they have not benefited as much as they could have from more specific positive feedback.

"Great job getting your foot on top of the ball for the volley on that great goal" is positive specific feedback and is incrementally more valuable for all the athletes on the team. The positive specific feedback shares exactly what went well about the movement. If the athlete knows what was effective about his or her performance, then it is easier for the athlete to repeat the performance.

When players know the process in achieving a good result, the positive feedback that they receive will result in a desire to repeat this movement. After the game, based on specific feedback, players might go home and work on getting their foot high and on top of the ball, when practicing the action on their own. Athletes feel better and learn more with positive specific feedback.

Examples of blanket positive feedback that are heard all the time are "Good job," "Great job," "Nice," "Great shot," "Great slap shot," "Awesome," and "There you go," do not really mean much to a player and relegates the coach to the role of cheerleader. "There you go" is actually confusing feedback as the athlete cannot always know what they did right, so knowing where they are going is confusing feedback. Blanket positive feedback can also lead to anxiety in very competitive situations. Anxiety is the word that we want all our athletes to avoid when competing.

For instance, a tennis player with a great serve, who can serve better than anyone on her team, with a coach who constantly puts her on a pedestal, verbally proclaiming and celebrating her great serve in practice, might feel good after she leaves every practice. When she plays in the state final and faces an opponent with a great return, this feedback can be confusing and detrimental for her. If all she has ever heard is knowledge of result feedback and that she is great at serving, she can doubt herself in more competitive situations, when other players are able to handle that serve.

The coach offering this type of generic positive feedback can be creating a fixed mindset in the athlete. The athlete is led to believe that her serving ability is almost an inborn trait. When she faces a superior competitor, she may crumble, feeling her inborn ability was not as great as she thought or was led to believe. Instead, the coach should constantly offer positive specific feedback which relates to exactly what is effective about her serve. The coach should also be telling the player what needs to be worked on to create an even more effective serve. In this way, the coach is leading the athlete to a growth mindset, realizing that the serve is based on effort and not inborn.

Positive specific feedback regarding that serve might sound like these statements, "great job rotating your hips" or "great wrist snap," reinforcing those skills for all the players. The player would be strengthened when she is facing a great returner, knowing that she can be effective serving against this great returner by focusing on what she does well, hip rotation and wrist snap. In fact, if she had only relied on the fact that she is a great server, when she was not in a situation that supported her coach's assessment, that would make her anxious and anxiety causes muscle tension which in turn would tense up her hips and wrist joints in turn decreasing range of motion in those joints and decreasing force production.

Blanket positive feedback will cause anxiety for competitors in competition. Realizing the coach had good intentions by using praise and the player enjoyed the praise, it is easy to see why inexperienced coaches fall into this trap. The more experienced coach will give positive specific feedback that gives the athlete praise and detailed information about the fundamental move. The athletes all learn more and they perform better in highly evaluative situations. Implement more positive specific feedback into your feedback as a coach and you will see immediate results.

CORRECTIVE FEEDBACK

Be careful when correcting a player's performance. All athletes come with their own personality. Their personality is as individualized as their fingerprint. All athletes react to feedback differently. A coach can say the same thing to two different players and get a different reaction from each player. Therefore, a coach must first get an idea of who they are talking to when they choose the words to use when providing feedback.

When giving corrective feedback, too much feedback might be difficult for some personalities to handle. The percentage of positive feedback and corrective feedback that athlete A can handle is different for athlete B. A coach has to know the player's personality to choose the level and nature of feedback that is best for each athlete. At some point, any athlete can be overloaded with too much corrective feedback. Sometimes coaches get too excited to share their knowledge and, in the process, they overload an athlete with too much corrective feedback.

You should have a goal of 80% positive feedback in your practices. Or for every corrective statement you should have five positive specific statements (5 to1). Not easy, especially when you are analyzing and giving corrective feedback to performers who are still learning. The performer might need a lot of corrective feedback because they are just learning a new skill or you could be an elite coach, who is dealing with an athlete who learned a bad habit. Be careful not to find yourself giving too much corrective feedback to try and correct old or incorrect movement patterns.

A good piece of advice for the elite coach is to not try to change movement patterns with bad habits, just tell the athlete that you are going to build a new movement pattern for that skill. A better approach would be to do it the old way, when you are playing outside of our team, but with us here, use this new move and you will love the results. This is a good way to avoid coaching headaches and to not confuse players about what is expected and why.

The fact is, when a coach is telling a player what they should do differently, this is categorized as corrective feedback, and it generally is not positive. Therefore, if a coach strives to have 80% positive feedback and a coach is doing a lot of teaching or correcting, he or she has a challenge before them. To inject more positive feedback into the player, and to keep the positive feedback specific, coaches should use what is called a *positive feedback sandwich* when correcting a performance.

A positive feedback sandwich is when a coach provides some positive specific feedback, followed by the corrective feedback and then closes the sandwich with another positive specific feedback. An effective way to approach this is to repeat the positive specific feedback. That makes the feedback easier for the coach and emphasizes what the athlete did well in the performance. The big takeaway is that in correcting a player's performance, the coach has now used 67% positive feedback with three statements. Add two more positive statements after the sandwich and the coach has now used four out of five positive feedback statements and reached the goal of 80% positive feedback.

An example of a positive feedback sandwich for a coach working with on correcting an athlete's arm swing when serving a volleyball is, "Great job tossing the ball out in front of you, but work on showing off more of your arm pit and keep that awesome toss." By wrapping the negative feedback in praise, the athlete feels the coach is giving constructive feedback, rather than negative criticism.

This can be especially true at the youth sport level where coaches are dealing with players who are more fragile to criticism and really need the positive feedback as beginning performers. This idea of a positive feedback sandwich is a great habit to get into as a coach. It is ok to repeat the positive statement in the first and third statement and in some ways better because it really emphasizes what is going well and makes the statement faster, taking less time.

It is very important that coaches work on communicating as much and as effectively as possible. The words we choose are the most valuable asset we have to modify a behavior or movement from our players. Therefore, it is extremely important for a coach to consistently evaluate and work on their feedback, what they are saying, and why they said it that way. Using your cell phone to record your practice is highly recommended.

From the recording, you can evaluate the amount of time your athletes were playing and listening (OTRs—Opportunities to Respond), you can tally your positive, corrective feedback, you can see if your positive feedback is blanket positive or specific positive. Finally, you can hear your tone and recognize any nuances that you are repeating and you can get the sense how enjoyable you are to listen to.

Once a coach has a great structure in place and the players buy into the core values, coaches can run practices that are time appropriate with well-structured activities, that increase motivation with competition or deliberate goals. When coaching staffs are well organized and speak the same language, adding effective communication, the participants will improve dramatically, but more importantly, the players will develop a love of the sport.

Working on your feedback is a key skill and no coach should ever stop evaluating how well they are providing feedback. A coach who gives effective feedback and communicates well with everyone on the team demonstrates competence and the athletes will know it from the first practice. Clear, honest communication is the best way to build a relationship in any setting.

SUMMARY

- Start to build relationships and the structure of the team by communicating the core values to the team.
- By communicating effectively your team culture will become positive and generate momentum toward your team's improvement. As well, your opponents will recognize your team's unique approach and it will shake their confidence.
- The coaching staff needs to communicate very well together to set an example for the team.
- Feedback is the skill that inexperienced coaches need to work on the most.
- Coaches should not talk long in practice and should avoid repeated nuances. Use your cell phone to evaluate what you say.
- Do not label players as good or not good. Rosenthal's research tells us what we think of our players will affect their performance.
- When giving feedback to players keep it simple and coach one cue at a time.

- Use a positive feedback sandwich when giving corrective feedback. This helps you achieve your goal of giving 80% positive feedback in practice.
- Use positive specific feedback. Blanket positive feedback can lead to your players feeling anxious.
- Feedback is a skill that all coaches need to work on continuously.

Chapter 7

Coaching Like a Teacher

Strategies That All Great Teachers Use That Will Improve Your Coaching

The best coaches are the best teachers. Teaching and coaching are the same thing. Therefore, to be an effective coach, you will need to perfect some excellent teaching strategies. My favorite saying as coach in regards to teaching and coaching is this: "Teaching and coaching are the same thing to me, it is just that volleyball is my favorite subject."

Many future professional coaches start their careers by majoring in physical education teaching majors as undergraduates. Learning how to manage a practice as a teacher in a classroom or gymnasium will help you immeasurably in coaching a team. Here are some tips to implement without having to get a degree in education.

INSTRUCTING

The most important thing a teacher does is plan. As a coach, you need to have a plan. A block plan with a list of items your team must be able do to over a certain period of time to play to their potential and a daily practice plan. Coaches know where they want their team to go but most do not plan on how they are going to get there.

Can you imagine a teacher not having a plan for the school year or semester and not having a lesson plan in the classroom? If an administrator saw that the teacher was instructing with no plan that teacher would not have a job for long. There is no way you are going to be successful as a coach without a plan. So many coaches go to practice without a plan. The first thing we need to do to emulate a teacher is plan like one. Here is how to carry out your plan.

As simple as this might sound, the coach first needs to know how to organize the team when giving instruction. Have the players line up on a line or in a specific area when you are giving instruction and be clear and consistent about the places. In a gym, you could have the team come in and line up on the baseline. On a soccer field, you could instruct the team to bring it in and stand in the center circle. You need to get the group together in an efficient and understood pattern, instead of a scattered mob, before you give any of the valuable information contained in your instruction. To have a group of youth sport participants just gather around without instruction on where and how to stand will lead to confusion and off-task behavior.

When you are instructing players, make sure no players are holding equipment. The equipment will distract the players. If a basketball coach is instructing the team how to shoot a jump shot, and during the instruction one of the players is bouncing a ball, this is very distracting to everyone and will undermine the instruction.

When instructing, have it as an expectation that the players will put the equipment on the ground in front of them, before you speak. Make it a practice to transition to instruction by putting the equipment away or just leaving it where they are before you begin speaking. For younger participants, you can use the expectation that there is "equipment, space, and you" to ensure players are not playing with the equipment when you are instructing.

Make sure that your back is never to any of the players when instructing. You want to be able to see everyone's eyes. If the team is in a circle, do not stand in the middle. Stand in the circle and give instruction to everyone's face. If someone is demonstrating, then make sure the demonstrator is in front of all the athletes so that they can see. For outdoor sports, make sure, as the coach, you are facing the sun and the players have their backs to the sun. You want all of the attention on you as a coach.

The instruction time should be packed with valuable information that you want to give to the player as quickly as possible to get them active and create more time for playing than listening. This is why you should practice your instruction before practice. That way, when you get in front of the team, you are polished and waste no time. Practices are for repetitions and not speeches. Conversations and lectures are better suited for the parking lot after practice.

Your instruction should consist of the skill and the important cue or cues the players will practice in that session, how the activity will be run, including a demonstration of the activity. You need to get points across clearly and quickly. Two to three minutes is all the time that this meeting should take. The coaches, who can avoid five- to ten-minute instruction time, will generate a lot more practice time over the course of a season. Plus, youth sport participants have spent an entire day listening to instruction in school and do not want to experience that in youth sports as well. Get the players practicing movement patterns as quickly as you can at the start of a practice.

Get your points across quickly, clearly, and effectively and, above all, avoid lectures. Organize your team when you are instructing so they can be in the best position to listen and understand. This is a skill that an experienced coach is very good at and one that sets a tone for an effective practice.

The experienced coach understands how important it is to get the players playing and has arrived at the most effective way to explain what will take place in the most efficient way. Players learn best when practicing, not listening. Remember, the most powerful learning tool is the image. You could skip your words by demonstrating with an expert performer and as few words as "bend your knees like this" and that would be immensely more effective than a coach talking for ten minutes on the parts of the skill.

TEACHING STYLES

We are all used to the "Command" teaching style that we have all been coached with and 90% of coaches use to run a practice. Command is basically, the coach says what to do and the players do it. The coach is making all decisions and controlling all aspects of the practice and the players are following. This is effective in many situations, especially when safety is a consideration, but realize there are different teaching styles that a coach could use to have their players learn. Here are the six pedagogical teaching styles that physical education teachers use that you could use to structure your practice.

1. Command—The coach makes all the decisions and the players follow
2. Practice—Students learn by carrying out the teachers described task (similar to command)
3. Self-Check—Students learn by assessing their own performance in comparison to the teachers' criteria
4. Inclusion—Students monitor his or her work throughout the lesson. Students choose at what level of difficulty to participate. The teacher makes modifications to the topic.
5. Reciprocal—Students learn by working in pairs: one performs while the other student provides feedback to the other. The teacher must never speak to the student performing. The teacher must speak to the student teaching and feed backing.
6. Guided Discovery—Students solve the teacher's movement problems with some assistance. Students are responded to objectives set forth through the teachers' questions.

Practice and command are very similar. Practice would be when a coach uses station work to practice various skills. An example of self-check is when a coach gives a deliberate goal and the team attempts to achieve that standard. Inclusion is interesting as by allowing players to choose what level of efficiency they would like to achieve the coach can get an understanding of what their level of self-belief is. This could help the coach encourage players to reach beyond what they believe their limits are. Reciprocal and Guided Discovery are two teaching styles that youth sport coaches need to take advantage of.

Reciprocal teaching style is when a coach sets up a scenario when the players teach each other. This is powerful because research has proven that players will listen to their peers more than they will listen to an adult. Also, by teaching the skill to another player and analyzing another player perform the skill, players who are giving feedback understand the skill better themselves.

An example of reciprocal teaching methodology is in swimming. The swimmer can be given five cues for the backstroke by the coach. Then as one swimmer is practicing the backstroke another swimmer is outside the pool with a checklist and checking off the cues the swimmer is doing well. At the end of the pool the observer can talk with the swimmer and review the cues that are going well and the ones the swimmer needs to work on.

When using the reciprocal teaching method, it is important that the coach not refine the swimmer's behavior. If there is a cue the observer is not noticing or the performer is not improving on, the coach should coach the teammate giving feedback. Do not diminish this powerful peer role by talking directly to the performer.

Guided Discovery is very powerful for youth sport participants. The teacher gives objectives for the players to achieve and the player discovers the proper cues on their own. A good youth baseball or softball example would be to line the player up in the outfield facing the home run fence. Using wiffle balls or tennis balls and hitting off a soft toss or a toss off a pitcher darting balls in on one knee, the player can be given the objective to hit three consecutive home runs. When the player makes three in a row she or he can back up 10 feet.

In attempting to generate power to hit the ball over the fence the coach will observe the players using great hip rotation and swinging from their core. Increasing force production might cause their head to move at which point the coach could be looking for this common mistake and modify that aspect of the skill. However, overall the players will be discovering how to generate more power by rotating their hips and torquing and keeping their weight transfer behind the ball. All good cues for batting that the players are discovering in attempts of achieving an objective given by the coach. This is very effective at the younger level.

Youth sport coaches should use various teaching or coaching styles like teachers do. Guided discovery is a great way for players to learn and learning on their own can equate to more retention. Especially, when a coach says "can you feel how much more power you are getting by swinging from your hips? Wow. Your hip rotation is awesome!" Use different teaching styles in your practice plans to increase your players' learning curve and give the session some variety to keep enthusiasm high.

ATTENTION GRABBER

You should have a consistent cadence that you use to get the players' attention. A whistle works well, but don't expect one whistle blast to get the players to stop moving. Three whistles could mean that your players should bring it in to get more instruction. For younger teams, the coach could blow the whistle once and then count down with "3–2–1 Freeze" with the expectation the players would all be still and listening on freeze.

At this point the coach could give further instructions to modify the activity, focus on another cue, or the coach could have the team come in for further instruction. Whatever communication system you use, everyone loves a good routine. Routine makes the environment predictable and the players know what is coming next. Establish a clear routine for transitions in practice so that no time need be wasted when moving from activity to activity or explaining or correcting.

TRANSITIONS

Transitioning from instruction to an activity and from one activity to another is important for a coach to plan with great detail. The more detail the coach has in the practice plan in regard to the transitions, the more effective the transitions will be. Coaches should, not only include what they are going to say in the transition, but they should also include what will be happening with the equipment. Coaches, who are inexperienced, spend a lot of time transitioning. The players lose activity time and the down time gives the players a chance to get off task.

Off-task behavior is anything the players are doing in place of focusing on the task at hand expected in the practice. When players are goofing around, talking or entertaining each other, usually the coach reacts with frustration. Ironically, the coach can avoid the off-task behavior through planning and implementing a more appropriate structure. Therefore, when players are off task, the coach should really be frustrated with their own planning.

Transitions are one of many good reasons why coaches should have a written practice plan that all the coaches understand before the practice session begins. The transition plans should include what you are going to say, what equipment is necessary, and what is the best way for the players to get or put away the equipment. If you are transitioning into station work, have the equipment ready at the stations where the activities are going to take place.

This seems simple, but it is not. Coaches need to plan with great detail to keep a great team structure in place during transitions. Being organized in transitions will also build your players' belief in you and your abilities as coach. Your attention to detail and organization affect the players' trust that you know what you are doing and are worth listening to in regard to how to play the game. You can also impact some of the youth sport participants who are not sure that they really like the sport, because they can feel your commitment and passion in regard to the sport. When planning a practice and transitions think of how every minute of the practice is going to go.

"When I say Go" is a great technique for a coach to use making his or her transition exciting and efficient. The coach can explain the skill and the important cues, give a great demonstration, explain the activity, and have the players ready to start and say, "When I say go you should get a partner and a ball and begin—"Ready—Go." That is a complete instruction and the players then transition into the activity with great enthusiasm.

A great teaching strategy that a coach can use at any level, including college, is the countdown. The team could be finishing an activity and the coach can employ an effective, "3–2–1 freeze" command. They players would stop and listen and at that point the coach might say, "When I say go, please put the balls in the bucket and line up on the first base foul line, and let's do that in ten seconds, Ready—Go." At which point, the coach could count down from 10, going faster or slower to help move the players, and at zero the transition should be over. This works with players at all levels, even the college level.

The countdown strategy really gets your players moving between activities, saves a lot of time, gives the players more time to play, and keeps the athletes focused on the practice and not on off-task behaviors. Any time the structure that you provide as a coach does not get the optimum performance out of the participants, you have to rethink that structure.

Be careful to avoid bringing your team in to talk and then pushing them back out to play too often. Too many of these transitions get boring and monotonous for the players. Instead, sometimes get your athletes to stop and listen where they are and just give the progression or new focus item (one at a time!) and then get them back into the activity. You have to use your *coach's voice* and yell loudly. Fortunately, your voice is a muscle that you can grow to effectively communicate over distance in ways that traditional teachers may never approach. When you are coaching loudly, accentuating the words helps your voice carry farther. Project your voice so the whole team can hear at times so that you do not lose the flow of the practice.

The way that you plan your transitions will affect the entire practice and team mindset. It is one of the most underdeveloped coaching skills at the youth sport level and above. It really stands out when a coach executes great transitions in his or her practices. The players get more time to be active and learn and really appreciate the organization that helps them focus and enjoy the sport more.

REFINING FEEDBACK BY CATCHING PLAYERS DOING THINGS RIGHT

As with all great teachers, when great coaches are giving feedback to modify a performance, they are refining the player's movement pattern. There are statements that you can use to help motivate the entire team to do better. You can catch players doing things correctly. "I like the way Latoya is following through when she is driving the ball." "I like the way Jill is moving her feet." "I like the way Georgie is running to get all the balls in." When a coach highlights these great performances, the other players will do the same in hopes of receiving positive feedback from the coach.

Catching players doing things right feedback not only sends a message to that player, but it resonates with the entire team. This is especially great at the youth sport level and early on in a season when you are working to have your team digest the core values. You can reinforce your core values in this way and the team will learn them faster.

CLOSURE

At the end of class, effective teachers make sure to review the important information that students worked on that day and so should coaches. Not a long meeting, but in three to four minutes, review your objectives of the day and what the players have learned. One way to do this is to ask questions and check for understanding. If you feel the players are comfortable with you, you can even call on different players to answer your questions. Closure is a good reminder of what the players have covered and improved on in the practice session.

For youth sports, it is a good idea to give a practice award during the closure. This award can be decided by the coaches and given to the player who best carried out the core values and who had a great attitude and stayed positive and connected to the objectives presented by the coaches. You can call this award anything that you choose. We have used the "Dude or Dudette of the Day Award" and of course you would introduce the winner by first stating there were a lot of great performances today and that made it difficult to just choose one player. With drama, end your practice, by saying in an overly theatrical voice, "the Dude or Dudette of the Day is . . ."

The closure time can also be used to give information about the upcoming schedule or what needs to be done to clean up before everyone leaves. A visual is good to use during practice and can be used at the end as well. For indoor sports if there is a white board that you can use to remind players of the cues used that day. You can also draw a diagram of the drill or plays that were run. Sometimes it is good to hang a poster board somewhere if you are coaching an outdoor sport. A white board or a poster board would be good to refer to during your closure. You can evaluate and assess what the players learned in your closure. A good evaluation in closure can help you prepare your next practice.

TIME

If there is not a clock in the facility, or your cell phone is not available, then you will need a watch. Try to stick to the assigned times in your practice plan. The flow of a practice is important. An experienced coach will know how much time to spend on an activity and how much is too little or too much time.

Teachers don't just do the same thing for a whole class or a whole day. The best teachers "chunk" lessons into ten-minute blocks to keep students engaged. Indoor scoreboards can count down time, but your phone works just as well. If you do not have the use of a scoreboard or you are outside then you set the timer on your cell phone and be disciplined enough to follow the assigned times even when the drill is not working optimally.

It is better to err on too little time for a drill than too much. It is always good to leave players wanting more rather than spending too much time on one activity until it gets boring. Finally, at the end of practice, you should be moving out of your part activities quickly to get the whole activity or modified games. This is where the real learning takes place and where you can assess the effectiveness of the day's teaching in game-like situations. If the players are not executing what you taught in your practice in a game situation, they have not learned it. The assessment from that scrimmage will help you effectively plan your next practice.

SUMMARY

- The best coaches are the best teachers.
- Have a clear plan for your team including block plans and practice plans.
- Do not have players play with equipment during instruction. It is distracting for the whole team.
- During instruction the coach should stand where all players can see him or her and the coach should face the sun.
- Keep instructions quick. It is not a lecture.
- Use a variety of teaching styles to improve players' learning curve. Try something other than the command teaching style.
- Use a consistent attention grabber.
- Plan for quick and organized transition times. Include in your practice plan how equipment will be handled.
- Use "when I say go" to transition from instruction to activity.
- Catch players doing things right.
- Use a closure to review what was taught and to check for understanding.
- Be aware of the time with a watch or cell phone. If you are using a cell phone you can use the timer to let you know when the time allotted for that activity is complete.

Chapter 8

Reactions to Errors

Let Errors Show Your Players the Path to Improvement

PRESENT

We know that the best way to play your best is to be focused on the present. Any time the focus of your thoughts is in the past or the future you are losing an opportunity to be completely invested on being your best right now. Your next actions are most important. Work on being your best now. Your past can help you prepare for the present but after you take your lessons learned from the past, stay present. Staying present will give you the most energy where your focus is best spent. Be present so you can eliminate distractions and stay connected to the objective. Being in the present gives you the most energy you need to be great at the next thing you are going to do.

With what we know about the present, how we handle errors from our athletes is most important. When coaches react negatively to errors they keep their own focus and the athlete's focus in the past. Errors are valuable to learn from. We need to celebrate our athletes' errors as an opportunity for understanding. As JFK once said, "a mistake is not a mistake until we fail to correct it." There is a lot to learn from the errors the athletes make on your team. It is important for coaches to have the correct perspective on the errors his or her athletes experience.

To build movement patterns from the brain to the body, it is not possible to learn a skill without making a mistake. How would you know what sweet tasted like if you did not experience sour? Your athletes need to go through a trial and error period to become expert performers. Therefore, be positive about the errors your athletes make. Just as you encourage them to see it as growth you have to believe this to be true. Your players' failures can be their fertilizer for success.

Also, sometimes when the athlete is performing a skill they execute the move fundamentally correct but the result is not there only because they are going too slow. You could be teaching a forearm pass in volleyball and the athlete executes all the skill cues but the ball goes behind them only because they made the move slowly. So many learners can get distracted by this failed result, and so do coaches. When learning the move, they are going slow. It won't take them long to make the move at game speed and then be successful in executing all the skill cues and the results come to fruition.

In these cases, the coach has to recognize that it was only the speed of execution that did not produce the result. The athletes are going to get frustrated so the coach has to be the one to instill confidence. The coach needs to reassure the athlete that that was a great move and to keep making that move so they can get used to it and move faster, at game speed. Sometimes this will come as soon as four or five repetitions. There is a great phrase that coaches can use in this stage of the learning process which is, "rather you be late than wrong."

Coaches should take it upon themselves to be responsible for the athlete's success and learning. Are the cues correct? Is the environment safe enough for the athlete to feel focused and comfortable learning? Am I spending the correct amount of time with the athlete or team on the skill that is not going well? Am I incorporating teaching tools like video and demonstrations to help any athletes learn the correct moves? Am I using corrective positive feedback sandwich when giving corrective feedback? Evaluate if you are giving the athlete the best chance to play to their potential.

Coaches should also realize that a large percentage of communication comes from their body language. That is why it is best for coaches to maintain consistent body language during good and bad times when coaching. If a coach is going to get really excited for a good play and have very negative reactions to a bad play, then the athlete will get the message very clearly that errors are not acceptable. Negative reactions to errors will cause athletes to have difficulty dealing with the anxiety and effect their next performance. Calm down. Take the emotion out of your communication. Easier to do if you are not concerned with winning or losing.

When an athlete does not have the opportunity to learn from the error and get ready for the next, they are not ready to perform. When a coach gets frustrated by an error and displays that in their body language or words, the athlete does not have the chance to move on from the error. Instead the athlete stays in the past. Since the athlete does not feel good about the past, they project to the future which is hard to imagine going well and overall, they are nowhere near having their focus in the present. If a player feels too negative about the error, they miss the opportunity to be at his or her best in the present moment.

INTENT

If you are having a challenging time thinking of something that went well when you are constructing your corrective positive feedback sandwich when giving corrective feedback, you can always comment positively on the effort. The athlete has shown up and is trying. Sometimes how much effort is really the most important thing a coach should be commenting about. That is another way to look at errors.

If the athlete was really focused and doing their best to make a great play and it didn't happen for whatever reason, there is no reason for a coach to show frustration. The athlete had great intent. If the athlete has great intent and the error occurs you really cannot be upset as a coach. If you are asking the athlete to do something they are not good at because you know it is what the athlete needs to improve their performance and the athlete is focused with great effort you cannot get upset as their coach. They won't trust you anymore.

Athletes that have great intent should be given praise, regardless of the result. When an athlete does not produce the result they are working on and then decides to keep working on that error, that's a good thing. Too many coaches, especially youth sport coaches do not have the patience to keep recognizing and rewarding the effort and intent. This athlete is the best thing that can happen to a coach and instead the athlete is receiving frustration over their failed result from their leader.

Frustration from the coach is valid if the athlete is frivolous and carefree with their focus in staying connected to the objective. This is the one time when the coach can react with some frustration. Most likely a good coach will have the expectation for focusing properly covered in their core values and they can refine the behavior by reminding the athlete of the core value they need to be more attentive of, getting the athlete back to performing skills with great intent.

Frustration usually comes from a coach because they know that their approach has been flawed. Frustration also usually occurs from a coach because they realize what they are doing is not successful. Dealing with the less experienced, less skilled player who does not seem to want to be involved is not easy. A coach must have a formula that works patiently with this player and motivates some part of the players' personality to give more effort. At the heart of every player is the fact that they want to do well. They want to be successful. Certainly, frustration and negative reactions are not going to make things easier.

Errors are an important statistic in any sport effecting winning and losing. Managing errors and the balance between risk and reward is important in many sports. For sure having anxiety about errors does not help them go away. The coach that has his or her basketball team run sprints for every free throw missed in a game is causing the athletes to make less than their potential. The tennis player who tells themselves "not to miss wide" is causing more errors. By focusing on what we do not want to happen causes the event more likely to take place. Coaches that react negatively to errors actually cause them to happen more.

Strategically, to avoid errors, it is better to think about a part of the process that you want to accomplish and be aggressive in making that happen. The basketball player could be keeping a majority of their thought on the target and using their legs. The tennis could be thinking about keeping their feet moving and snapping the top spin. Both more beneficial thoughts that are hard to keep in mind if a coach is reacting negatively to errors. Not only have positive thoughts but be aggressive. Eliminating hesitation by reacting positively is a great way to let the performer play freely.

When a coach comments negatively with either negative body language or their feedback after a player has an error and the player had great intent to practice a new move or work on a new strategy, this coach is not serving the athlete well. At the same time the coach that gets over excited about the positive result, even when the fundamental move was flawed, is also giving improper feedback. Coaches who ask for change and then get mad at the result when it is negative are debilitating the athlete's progress. We need to have our athletes become comfortable with failing in practice so they can learn how to improve.

One great feedback line to use with an athlete after an error is "Tell me what you thought about that play and I will tell you what I think." This statement helps the coach understand what the athlete's intent was. Also, after hearing the athlete's thoughts the coach can provide a learning opportunity for the player who is confused. Sometimes the youth sport athlete will have no idea what the correct thought is in a particular situation and then this becomes a great learning opportunity.

Think of a young athlete that has their first big failure. What a great opportunity to be their coach. For example, maybe one of your star players who has made every penalty kick the entire season has a chance to win the championship with a PK and for the first time in her or his career misses! This could be that person's most important and memorable failure. As their coach you have a chance to mold their future and how they approach other such failures that will occur in life. At that moment you could be the one to provide this young person the framework for all their future success! A huge opportunity not to be handled insensibly.

If the error was brought upon because of anxiety or being distracted then as their youth sport coach you have the ability to evaluate about how to focus on the process. If the error was a result of the child thinking about winning or losing and missing the opportunity to focus on the present you have the ability to direct their attention toward practicing so this error does not happen again. This could help all their future big pressure moments in sports and life. Part of the responsibility of being called "Coach."

If your team is making a few too many errors during competition and especially in bigger competitions, this may be happening because of a cultural failure. The behaviors and actions of the players not enabling the team to play to their potential and that is because the cultural demands are not clear. Usually these off-task behaviors and actions have to do with improper direction toward winning and losing or relationships between players or between players and coaches. Players or coaches are not building relationships necessary with respect and good communication that enable the team to play anxiety free and to their potential. Again, these expectations should be clear in the core values to avoid cultural failures.

Athletes who embrace failure and push themselves to get better with great intent should be rewarded. These positive behaviors should be recognized and highlighted by coaches, especially at the youth sport level. There could be a post practice recognition of the "dude" or "dudette" of the day recognizing the player who handled errors the best. This recognition could go highlight any of the core values of the team.

When a coach builds a culture that reacts to errors with the proper mindset, everyone enjoys the environment more and errors occur less often. By avoiding reacting negatively and harshly to player' errors with verbal feedback or negative body language, the athletes are more comfortable. Remember the number one reason youth sport athletes are there is to have fun. Today with the increased pressure that social media has on all of our young athletes, mental health is more highlighted at every level of sport. When the focus is growing as people and players and everyone working toward their potential rather than winning or losing, everyone is more comfortable.

Encourage your athletes to race toward failure. Practice should not be so easy only performing the skills you can do. That moment when youth sport athletes need to learn something new is so important in their development. As their coach, be their guide. Enjoy this opportunity. Calm things down for the kids and help them feel comfortable. This is where the real growth happens. Don't ruin this moment with a negative response.

SUMMARY

- Errors are essential for learning.

- By handling errors properly coaches keep the athletes' focus in the present.
- Athletes' frustration has to be met with coach's composure.
- Coaches communicate a lot with body language.
- There is no such thing as a bad error if the player had good intent.
- Focusing on what we don't want to do will cause athletes to do it more often. Instead players should focus on being aggressive about what they want to do.
- Errors, especially big ones, early in a players' development are huge opportunities for learning.
- Build a culture through your core values that reacts to errors with a proper mindset.
- When learning new skills, race toward failure.

Chapter 9

Game Day

Things to Consider When Preparing for Competition

PREPARATION

In the same way that practice routines are essential for successful practices, game day routines are just as vital for game days. These routines have to be practiced with as much emphasis as are the drills that define your practice. The key to establishing these routines is for the coach to prepare for all of the situations that may arise.

Coaches must be mentally prepared to . . .

- Handle your players failing.
- Have to repeat something you have already said a million times.
- Reward a great effort and feedback about the process.
- Reinforce and refer to your core values and be prepared to be excited.
- Act out and choose behaviors that reflect your team's core values and everything you believe in.

Leaders in every field need to be able to answer the question, "who is leading you?" This same question must be answered by every coach who hangs a whistle around their neck. This is challenging for all coaches, but especially youth sport coaches.

It is not easy to leave the stress of a job and jump onto the field and lead in a whole new arena. A coach's real job is the most defining thing that they do in life and making the transition to become a youth sport leader at the end of the day is no easy feat. Many youth sport coaches are sacrificing time from work to coach and may find it difficult to leave the office stress behind.

Suddenly, coaches must transform and become holistic youth sport coaches. This is no easy task. Coaches must be prepared to compartmentalize that part of their life and leave any frustrations that come along with it behind, when they put their coach's hat on. Although most coaching positions are volunteer positions, this does not make them any less demanding.

Preparing the game day lineup and a plan for involving all of your players is a major responsibility of the coach. Many leagues will have requirements on how much every player has to play and demands that players must play multiple positions. Therefore, the starting point must be to ensure that all the league requirements are met. It is really challenging when a player does not show up and you have to redo the entire line-up at the site.

Although making a lineup may sound simple, it can lead to stress and confusion as the coach may be torn between putting the strongest team on the field and ensuring that league and participation requirements are met. It is difficult to find the balance between these concerns and coaches can err by being too extreme in either capacity, trying to build a line-up to win or trying to build a lineup that insures everyone is going hope happy.

It is important to communicate with parents and require parents to inform you in advance if their son or daughter is not going to be there so you can be organized. In sports such as basketball or soccer, the coach should plan for when the substitutes are going to go in and who they are going to go in for.

When preparing lineups, the coach should attempt to ensure the best combination of players is in place so that the lineup is able to put every player in a position to be successful, while trying to maintain a successful team result. You have to know when the lesser skilled players are in and make sure that you balance team strength so that both team and individual goals can be met. It is generally not a good idea to substitute your most struggling players all at once, unless this is coordinated with the other coach.

You also want to strategically give players playing time in a position that they are going to have the best chance to succeed. Again, lesser skilled or players with less enthusiasm need to feel great in your culture and you want to put them in positions that will get them excited about their progress. To coach these players is the greatest challenge for most youth sport coaches. This effort takes a lot of time and planning, but when these players develop in practices defined by great process and have success in competitions, it will be the most important rewarding aspect of coaching young athletes.

COMMUNICATING WITH PARENTS

One coach on the team should take on the responsibility for communicating with the parents. My recommendation is that this should be the only one person that sends communications. That way, the parents get used to seeing the email from that coach, recognizing the email address, and immediately knowing that the message pertains to the team. Parents would then know who to contact when their child cannot make a game. This coach should be the coach with the most organized and consistent communication skills.

The principle of letting the coaches know when an athlete cannot attend, or if they are going to be late, also applies to practice. Explain that as a volunteer coach you are planning out practices to be as efficient as possible and not starting on time or changing groups that you have planned for in practice because a player has not shown or shows up late takes away from the quality of the practice.

Communicate well in advance with parents and, in the same way that you expect their children to be on time and let you know in advance when they cannot attend, it is vital that coaches make sure they are on time. Coaches need to set an example, setting up the field and getting out the equipment before the practice starts.

One coach should also be communicating any cancellations or changes in schedule with the parents. This news needs to be emailed or texted to the parents. Keep the emails short. Do not write an essay about how well the team is growing in an email unless it is the final email. Use bullet points to make your emails more understandable. Get to the point in your emails and be sure you communicate what the parents need to know.

Communicating with parents seems like just another burden on your growing to do list, but it will be really helpful to communicate really well at the start of a season so you don't need to communicate much at the end. You can save a lot of work by getting out in front of communication with parents. That is why it is a good idea to share in an email at the start of the season what your purpose is in being the coach, what your expectations are, and maybe even what the core values are so that parents are familiar with them. By sharing a bit of your purpose and structure and expectations, parents can do their job of being supportive. Everyone has a part to play in the team's success.

It is also essential that you communicate clearly game day expectations for parents. It is essential that you explain what values and behaviors that will not be tolerated in regard to referees. Often the referees are young student volunteers and parents get confused, demonstrating the poor sportsmanship towards a young referee. This behavior is not acceptable at any level, but sportsman-like behavior must be nonnegotiable at youth level. Before your first game have this talk with parents and clearly lay out consequences for such behavior.

At this meeting, also communicate the fact that parents are not to attempt to coach their child on the sidelines. Try to explain that you have coached their child to do certain things and their sideline coaching will only confuse the child. Does the child obey their parent or do what it is that they have been coached to do in practice sessions? Explain to them that this behavior, above all, will not be tolerated. If they persist in trying to coach from the sidelines, they will be removed from the game site.

PLAYER'S ROLE

Give each player a role on game day and clearly communicate that role with them. Players appreciate clarity in what the expectations are, in order to know they have a part in the team success and will perform better if the coach explains their role with them. When a player buys into their role, even if it is not a glorious one, they will play to their potential and the team benefits.

The Chicago Bull's dynasty was amazing to watch. One of the most amazing things was to watch how every player on the roster was important and how the coach Phil Jackson emphasized to each player how important they were. It was amazing to see how many games the Bulls won where their opponent would do a good job defensively holding Jordan and Pippen but would still lose. This was because every player on the Bulls was prepared to execute their role.

During a Bull's game, it was not unusual that somewhere in the third quarter some journeyman player for the Bulls, no one would remember his name, would come off the bench, substitute into the game, only play three minutes but would have three rebounds, a steal, and eight points! This player would be prepared to fulfill the minimal role he had and recognize its importance. The result was that it was difficult to beat the Bulls, no matter what success you had with Jordan and Pippen. It was amazing to observe Coach Jackson get everyone excited about their role and how important it was to the team's success.

In the same manner that you give everyone a role in team success, be sure to give everyone a role in setting up for a game or practice. The roles should have to do with markers, equipment, water, or the first aid kit. Assigning these roles, and rotating these roles, will not only teach your players about responsibility, but it will make your life a lot easier every game day. Be sure to put these in writing on a white board or in an email.

COACHING/TEACHING DURING COMPETITION

Be careful not to try to teach too much during competition. At the professional level, a coach is not doing any teaching during the competition. Competing for an athlete is about having confidence that you can make the next play under any circumstances and trusting your ability. If a coach is teaching the player how to perform during competition, the athlete can begin to doubt their ability.

The athlete has to trust the game they brought to the competition and believe and trust in their ability. A good coach at the professional level would only be giving tactical information and support during a competition. If this is true at the professional level, you can only imagine how important it is for you to follow at the youth level.

Training is totally different for professional and youth athletes. Training is when an athlete learns and repeats movement patterns so they become part of their automatic subconscious. If something did not go well during the competition, the athlete should be working on getting repetitions on that skill in practice. It is hard to reverse those patterns in a game without practice repetitions.

Training and competing in a game require separate mindsets. Great players don't work on their game during competition, they trust their game. By over coaching a player during competition, the coach may be creating doubt in the player, moving the player away from a confident, trusting mindset to one that is plagued by self-doubt.

When coaching a younger or novice athlete during a competition, it is challenging not to teach them because the situations they are experiencing can be brand new to them. There are many learning opportunities that come about during a competition at the youth sport level but try to make sure you are giving some room to learn for themselves during competition, this often includes making errors.

A youth sport coach should not micromanage everything that happens in a competition. A coach needs to let the athlete make their own decisions to help them grow. A youth sport coach can teach at points during a competition, but make sure to observe and support as well. Use the lessons and mistakes in a game as the template for training and learning in the following practice session.

The conversations in practice about situations that occurred in the game are great opportunities for the coach to teach an athlete as well as to build relationships. The coach has a chance to support and bond with the player and then be a resource for the players' improvement. The coach who is process orientated will regard games and competition opportunities for growth and learning.

The coach who is result orientated might still be upset about the loss and the team moving down in the standings, but that should not be case. If the youth sport coach can walk the line between giving some instruction during competitions and letting the athlete experience errors, followed by support in practice, the athlete will improve, and success will follow. The end game of youth coaching is not a championship trophy, but the growth of the individuals on your team and increase in their love of the game.

WINNING

Be prepared to deal that the reality of youth sports in America is often measured in results, standings, and championships. Too many parents are only concerned with success on the next level of play and even dreaming of college scholarships, even for athletes as young as eight years old. Be prepared to shelter your team from that reality and to remind your team to focus on the things they can realistically control, including effort, confidence, belief in their ability, and preparation. Instead of final scores, stress how they communicate and connect with the team's objectives and their role on the team. Teams will always be successful if they adopt that mindset.

Try to create an environment in which players are playing for fun, respecting their opponents, being relaxed, and giving their best physical and mental effort. Stress that real winning involves helping others on their team, and they do not need to associate their self-value with the score so that they can enjoy and learn the process. Instill in your athlete that they often have no real control over the end product, only of their effort.

The same is true for you as coach. Your self-value is not associated with the end result of a game. This competition is not you vs. the opposing coach. If you have structured your team correctly and you have laser focus on the process, guess what, you always win in the end. The side bonus is that if you have done all that result takes care of itself. Enjoy!

COACHES COMPETING

Be ready for the coach who wants to be very competitive with you. There is going to be a coach who is very hands on with his or her team. They are going to be very vocal and will be attracting a lot of attention. They could be yelling loudly and highlighting their actions. They will have a different purpose for taking the coaching position than you do. Sometimes, they are going to have a better team made up of more talented players than you do and your team is going to lose to their team. Remember, your self-worth is not associated with how good your team is or how much better of a coach you are than this coach.

Do not get caught up in competing with this coach. Your players are most likely distracted by this coaches' antics. By focusing on your competition with this coach you are losing an opportunity to direct your players' attention to what is important. At a time when your players need you. Remain connected with your core values and the purpose of competing. Some youth sport coaches get frustrated they are losing and start to react negatively to their players. Choosing anger and reacting to the scoreboard will take you away from your goals as a coach.

Keep the focusing on doing the best for your team. Especially when you are losing on the scoreboard. In the long run, caring for your players is more important than competing with another coach. Remember at any level, coaching is not about you. It is about structuring a great team with many learning opportunities for the participants. Keeping your composure and sticking to your core values, will enable your players to win the big game.

SUMMARY

- Prepare for game day organization such as lineups and prepare to have a great mindset.
- Make the sometimes-difficult transition from the stress of work. Compartmentalize work and coaching.
- Communicate with parents so you know what players are going to be present for the competition.
- Communicate well with parents.
- Define each player's role and communicate to all the players on the team.
- Give the athlete space to learn and comfort to perform on game day. Minimize coaching and wait to teach skills in the next practice.
- Don't fall to the pressure of winning. Don't react to the scoreboard.
- Don't compare, compete, and coach vs. the opposing coach. Keep your energy toward your team and being process orientated with your team.

Chapter 10

Youth Sports in Norway

Are We Moving in the *Right Direction?*

The last Olympic Games in South Korea, Norway won more medals than any other country in history of the winter Olympics. Norway won more Gold, Silver, and Bronze medals than any other country before had and had almost twice as many total medals than the United States. Not bad for a country that has the same population of the greater Boston area. How did that happen? Was that the result of intense training at the youth level, rigorous training teams, and selective early national teams? No, quite the opposite!

Norway has a very specific youth sport system and it offers a dramatic example for our culture in American of what sports could be for all children. The country follows the same policies for all fifty-four of its youth sports. Not only has Norway done well in winter sports, but recently the men's soccer team has been remarkably successful in international competitions.

Two of its athletes are now being heralded as international superstars. Erling Haaland, in 2019, was rated second in the "Top 20 most valuable young footballers in Europe." A twenty-one-year-old beach volleyball player, Anders Mol, was nominated by the international volleyball federation as the "most outstanding player in 2018." Both these international stars are products of the youth sport system in Norway. Not only is Norway producing great winter Olympic athletes, which makes sense because of the climate in Norway, they are also producing world class players in summer Olympic sports as well. What is remarkable is that these athletes are products of a youth sport system that is polar opposite in style and substance to the system we use in America.

These world class results, coming from one of the smallest countries in the world, have a youth sport system that does not emphasize winning. At the earliest levels, the system does not even want to acknowledge who or what team has won. There are no youth sport national championships before the age of thirteen and no regional championships in any sport before the age of eleven.

No championship trophies and awards ceremonies are permitted in Norway. Leagues do not allow MVP awards, all-star teams, and there are no medals, ribbons, or trophies at all. Before the age of eleven, there are no league standings. Compared to a system in America, driven by an AAU National Basketball Championship in grades as young as second grade, these provide a stark contrast. In America, there is even a third-grade national top prospect list in basketball.

The country's youth sport philosophy is spelled out in a document called "The Children's Rights in Sports." All 54 youth sports have to follow the rules of this document or they will not receive any funding or support from the national council. The document is produced by the Norwegian Olympic and Paralympic committee and conference of sports.

The document gives expectations that every youth sport participant must be given the right to decide and plan their own sport activities and children decide how much they would like to train. Attendance is not mandatory and children can decide what club they want to play for. If a child decides he or she would like to change clubs in the middle of the season, no problem.

Since there is no National or Regional championship there is not a lot of travel and cost of participation is so low that all children can participate. As a result, 93% of children in Norway play a youth sport. For those children who are performing better and would like to, they can move on to a more competitive environment after the age of thirteen and receive professional coaching.

At fifteen years of age, when 70% of kids are dropping out of sports in the United States, the athletes in Norway are just starting to specialize more and train more hours, now with more intense competition. The Norwegian counsel of sport believes this model is better for the development of the participants mentally and physically.

The motivation of the kids is the most important quality highlighted in the youth sport document in Norway. The approach focuses on the children being satisfied and happy. One reason why the country adopted this model is because since they are such a small country they could not afford to lose any participants. Even the participants who are not the best performers at the age of eight are needed for league play.

The model suggests that the participants who are not performing well at early ages can grow to be better performers as they mature. Their skill set often develops at the age of thirteen when their body changes significantly. The fact that children perform a variety of sports helps them to become more well rounded and avoid overuse injuries and burnout. The Norwegian model keeps the athlete's passion burning by avoiding stress, anxiety, and pressure from parents and coaches.

One big difference in our countries is that universities are free in Norway. Without having to pay for college, Norwegian athletes are not hiring private coaches and getting extra strength and conditioning sessions in before thirteen in hopes of earning an athletic scholarship. Moving on to the next level and making the elite, premier, or travel team does not exist as a goal for college scholarship. It is truly a Montessori educational approach to youth sports. The participants play what they want, when they want, and for how long they want. The model focuses on having fun and recreating with friends.

The results are evident. The United States is not lacking in funding for winter Olympic sports, nor top rated training facilities. What is lacking is a fundamental approach to align with the needs and desires of the participants. Yes, by not focusing on winning, the youth sport approach in Norway leads to more winning. This approach gives attention to a process of teaching the kids to compete in all the items they can control in sports, choosing to be confident, understanding and building movement patterns, mental and physical effort, persevering when success is difficult, communicating and striving together with friends, and having fun.

Inge Anderson, the former secretary general of the Norwegian Confederation, told the *New York Times*, "It's impossible to say at eight or ten, who is going to be talented in school or sports (Norway uses a similar model in education). That takes another ten years. Our priority is the child becoming self-reflective about their bodies and minds." A philosophy that does not put being the best in your sport or winning as a priority at early ages seems to have more long-term success on every level. Maybe we could learn a lot from Norway.

To learn more about Youth Sports in Norway go to YouTube and search "Norway Youth Sport Model." Watch the three-minute video with Brian Gumbel, "The Norwegian Way." One youth coach, a volunteer with a doctorate degree, when asked why some kids are more talented than others maintains he does not like the word, "talent." "Those who are more talented have been skiing since they were young. Those, who are not as talented, have just started, but if they kept skiing, they would not be very different than the more talented ones at age fifteen."

The ski program cost sixty dollars for six months. It is difficult to buy a daily ski pass for less than sixty dollars in America, let alone get instruction for six months, included in that cost. The participants are asked to pay once. and if they cannot pay, they are not asked again. Their child continues to participate with or without payment. There are races, but no results are posted. Instead, there is a lot of fun. Without much formal homework in Norway, the kids and the entire community ski most nights after dinner from seven to nine.

As youth sport coaches, we can all learn a lot from the youth sport model in Norway. We can slow down on pushing the kids to play at a certain level and worry less about winning at a younger age. Our teams can eliminate the tournaments on weekends that require the team's families to buy plane tickets, get hotels, incurring a large additional cost that leave out the less fortunate.

Maybe qualifying for the world championship in Dublin, Ireland for Irish dancing is less important than your kid having a great time and wanting to participate in Irish dance next year.

We can learn that as youth sport coaches and coaches at every level have the responsibility to take care of the participants' well-being. We can create an environment that is safe for all participants and support all those who call us "Coach." We have to emphasize the process and not get caught up in the societal vortex of winning. Winning at all costs is costly for all. For sure, the system that is used in the United States produces athletes that dominate on the world stage, but we could produce more and the system could produce more well-rounded and participants who are building life skills to be successful.

Matt Anderson is a player on our USA Men's Volleyball National Team. The Rio Olympics was his third Olympic games and at the time that the team competed in Rio, Matt was easily one of the best three, if not the best player in the world. Matt also was a star player for the best professional club team in the world in Kazan, Russia. How did Matt develop into such an amazing volleyball player coming out of our youth sports volleyball program? The answer may surprise you.

Matt did not play volleyball at a young age. Matt played other sports at a young age. What is amazing to think about is that Matt's first year of playing volleyball was his sophomore year in high school. If Matt had been competing for a national championship and had the pressure of winning in fourth grade, maybe he would not have turned into the great volleyball player he eventually became. Matt's success speaks not only to his extraordinary ability, but seems to support this Norwegian concept of focusing on the joy of participating in multiple sports while young and concentrating with more intense focus at later ages.

The Norwegian youth sport model provides an excellent pathway for us to learn how to be effective youth sport coaches in America. Taking the strengths from the Norwegian system, and applying those practices in our youth sports would help us regain our sanity and provide an overall more enjoyable experience for all. Coaches, players, parents, referees, leagues, and even spectators could all enjoy being part of a system that was more process orientated than product orientated.

In Norway, youth sports seem to be getting it right. Sports serves all types of participants. Surely, not everyone that participates in the ski program aspires to be in the Olympics. Those who have such aspirations, still have the opportunity to grow into well-rounded international superstars. Norway doesn't expose children to a parent's goal of winning a national championship or earning a scholarship to stress them out they are in fifth grade.

Although it is unlikely that we are going to reverse our national sports philosophy in America, we can all learn from Norway's example as parents and youth coaches. We can tone down the noise about winning, scholarships, travel teams, and personal trainers. We can all return to focus on what is really important about playing youth sports. We can rediscover why children play sports. In case, you forgot, it can be summed up in one word, **FUN!**

About the Author

Charlie Sullivan is the head men's volleyball Coach and Professor of Physical Education at Springfield College. He is the co-author of *Winning the Game of Belief, Cultivating the Cultural Grit that Defines America's Greatest Coaches.* Charlie has won 11 National Championships at Springfield College and he is the winningest coach in the history of Div. III Men's Volleyball. In 2015 Charlie was awarded the "All Time Great Coach" award by USA Volleyball. Sullivan has won the AVCA Div. III National Coach of the Year award four times. The Springfield College men's volleyball team has produced more Player of the Year, Newcomer of the Year, and All-Americans under Sullivan's guidance than any other college team. Charlie has worked as a consultant coach for the USA men's volleyball team and recently was part of the Bronze Medal team at the Rio Olympics in Brazil.

www.ingramcontent.com/pod-product-compliance
Lightning Source LLC
Chambersburg PA
CBHW032029230426
43671CB00005B/254